P9-ARF-990

The Travel Narratives
of Ella Maillart

TRAVEL WRITING ACROSS THE DISCIPLINES

THEORY AND PEDAGOGY

Kristi E. Siegel
General Editor

Vol. 12

PETER LANG
New York • Washington, D.C./Baltimore • Bern
Frankfurt am Main • Berlin • Brussels • Vienna • Oxford

Sara Steinert Borella

The Travel Narratives of Ella Maillart

(En)Gendering the Quest

PETER LANG
New York • Washington, D.C./Baltimore • Bern
Frankfurt am Main • Berlin • Brussels • Vienna • Oxford

Library of Congress Cataloging-in-Publication Data

Borella, Sara Steinert.
The travel narratives of Ella Maillart: (en)gendering the quest / Sara Steinert Borella.
p. cm. (Travel writing across the disciplines: theory and pedagogy; vol. 12)
Includes bibliographical references and index.
1. Maillart, Ella, 1903–1997. 2. Travel writers—Switzerland—Biography.
3. Travelers' writings, Swiss (French). 4. Travel writing—History. I. Title.
G154.5.M346B67   915.04'41'092—dc22   2005022525
ISBN 0-8204-6388-4
ISSN 1525-9722

Bibliographic information published by **Die Deutsche Bibliothek**.
Die Deutsche Bibliothek lists this publication in the "Deutsche
Nationalbibliografie"; detailed bibliographic data is available
on the Internet at http://dnb.ddb.de/.

Cover art provided by the Musée de l'Elysée/Fonds Ella Maillart, Lausanne.

The paper in this book meets the guidelines for permanence and durability
of the Committee on Production Guidelines for Book Longevity
of the Council of Library Resources.

© 2006 Peter Lang Publishing, Inc., New York
29 Broadway, New York, NY 10006
www.peterlangusa.com

Printed in Germany

To my parents

Table of Contents

Acknowledgments

Special thanks go to my colleagues at Pacific University, especially the members of the department of World Languages and Literatures, for their enthusiastic support of this project over the years. Professor Lorely French discussed many of the ideas in this book with me in addition to reading much of it. Her help has been invaluable. Heartfelt thanks to Laura Lynch and Caitlin McCool for reading and rereading my drafts. I am especially appreciative of the continued support of Anneliese Hollmann in Geneva, who graciously gave her advice on this project in its various stages. Daniel Girardin, curator at the Musée de l'Elysée in Lausanne, generously provided the cover photo of Ella Maillart (1934) with permission of the museum and Anneliese Hollmann. I would also like to express my thanks to Françoise Pittard at the Bibliothèque Publique et Universitaire in Geneva for her continued expert council through all stages of my research. Likewise, I wish to thank Pacific University and Franklin College Switzerland for their support of my research and the publication of this book. At Peter Lang, my editor Phyllis Korper has shared her insight and excellent suggestions. Finally, none of this would have come together without the fine technical advice of Maria Amorso.

Two chapters of this book have derived from previously published articles. Thus, I gratefully acknowledge Catherine Montfort, executive director of *Women-in-French Studies* as well as Corinna Moldava, director of *Agora* for their permission to print revised versions of "Re-Discovering the Travel Narratives of Ella Maillart" (*WIF Studies*, 2001) and "La voyageuse, le voyageur et le regard de l'autre" (*Agora*, 2003).

In closing, I could not have completed this work without the constant encouragement of my family. My love and thanks to Pietro, Anna, and Miriam, without whose unending support and enthusiasm this project would never have reached completion.

Chapter One

Re-Discovering the Travel Narratives of Ella Maillart

Ella Maillart's noteworthy life story might tempt any aspiring biographer: born in Geneva in 1903, her travels and adventures earned her an impressive series of headlines for decades both at home and abroad. Member of the Swiss national ski team, intrepid mountaineer, Swiss Olympian in the 1924 summer games, and accomplished sailor, Maillart won races and set new milestones for women athletes. She worked as a teacher, cabin hand, first mate, stunt person, photographer, journalist, and writer. Fluent in French and English with a good command of German and Russian, the self-taught Maillart traveled the world. She walked across the Caucasus in 1930, traveled to the far reaches of Russian Turkistan in 1932, crossed China from Peking to the Himalayas in 1935, and drove across Afghanistan in a brand new Ford shortly before the outbreak of the Second World War. Even more fascinating than her extraordinary biography are the travel books she wrote about her experiences. Maillart recounts through her prose and photos the stories that made up these journeys; her travel books offer observations and images of worlds little known to her readers. Perhaps more importantly, they reveal much about the construction of the self and the Other at a time when European colonialism was literally running out of room. Maillart's six travel books and her autobiography make a significant contribution to the larger body of women's travel writing and to feminist studies as a whole. Yet outside of Switzerland, Ella Maillart remains virtually unknown to the scholarly world.[1] The New York Times devoted more than a quarter page to her obituary in 1997, attesting to her fame. Her travel books were best sellers in the 1930s and 1940s. Given this extensive biography and renown, why do Ella Maillart and her travel books linger in the margins of French literary studies?

In Maillart's case, I would argue that three specific factors have contributed to her near disappearance from the literary scene: her Swiss identity, the genre of the travel narrative, and gender. First, Maillart's Swiss origins make it especially difficult to situate her work on the literary map of the twentieth century. Switzerland's relative literary obscurity as well as the country's problematic relationship to the rest of colonial Europe makes an analysis of Maillart's travelogues especially complex. Second, the simple fact that Maillart wrote travel books complicates her place in literary history. As Michael Kowalewski observes in his introduction to *Temperamental Journeys: Essays on the Modern Literature of Travel*, "There is a venerable tradition of condescending to travel books as a second-rate literary form" (2). Is travel writing, as Paul Fussell would suggest, a lost genre, one that disappeared with the advent of the Second World War? [2] If not, has post-colonial travel literature and criticism so changed the way we read that there is no longer a place for writers like Maillart, positioned precariously between the colonial and post-colonial worlds? Finally, where do women fit into this problematic genre? In a colonial enterprise that wrote the equation explicitly for men (where men are the colonizers and the unknown, exotic other becomes the colonized), women are virtually erased from the picture. Despite women's participation in and writing about the colonial world, much colonial criticism has ignored women's roles and contributions. Sara Mills emphasizes the importance of the conflict between women's discourse and colonial discourse in her critical study *Discourses of Difference* when she writes: "Women's travel texts are constructed in the process of interaction of colonial textual constraints and constraints of gender" (40). How does Maillart, who as a Swiss writer of the 1930s and 1940s exists in the margins of this colonial discourse, make a place for herself? How should we read Maillart's travelogues? This introduction and the chapters that follow will work to answer these very questions, first examining a national and colonial context in which to read Maillart's texts and later examining Maillart's texts themselves. Finally, this study will situate Ella Maillart among other women travelers of the era in an effort to create a context in which to (re)read and (re)locate her forgotten travel narratives.

In the domain of Swiss literature, Maillart belongs, in fact, to a long tradition of wanderers and writers. Nicolas Bouvier,[3] her compatriot and near contemporary, argues in his *L'Echappée belle: éloge de quelques pérégrins* that this self-imposed exile is practically a national trait for the Swiss: "il y a . . .dans notre histoire une constante de nomadisme, d'exil, de quête, d'inquiétude, une manière de ne pas tenir en place qui ont profondément marqué notre mentalité et donc, notre littérature. Il y a, depuis deux mille ans, une Suisse vagabonde, pérégrine, souvent jetée sur les routes par la pauvreté et dont on parle trop rarement" (13).[4] [There is...in our history, a nomadic constant, one of exile, quest, worry, a way of not remaining in one place that has profoundly touched our mentality and hence, our literature. There is, and has been for 2000 years, a vagabond, wandering Switzerland, one often thrown out on the road by poverty and of which we speak too rarely.][5] In the modern tradition, Blaise Cendrars, the Swiss-French poet and novelist, figures as a mainstay in Swiss travel writing with *La Prose Transsibérien* (1913), *Feuilles de route* (1924), and *Bourlinguer* (1948).[6] Likewise Bouvier, the author of numerous travel books including *L'usage du monde* (1963), *Chroniques japonaises* (1975) and *Le Poisson-Scorpion* (1982), contributes to this tradition. Maillart shared the Swiss restlessness of which Bouvier speaks. In the Swiss multilingual community, these writers clearly make up a French-speaking minority, yet they are not French. Even within that French-speaking minority, another Swiss characteristic that has been systematically institutionalized works to disenfranchise Maillart from her compatriots: men write and men travel, thus assuring male agency and authority. Historically, and until recently enough politically, Swiss women have been excluded from this paradigm. With women only gaining the vote nationally in 1971, they have effectively been excluded from a variety of public arenas, including authorship. Maillart thus writes from the margins, even doubly so, as a Swiss French author in a German-speaking majority and as a woman writing against a well-defined, patriarchal tradition.

This is not to say that Swiss women do not write. Today, women are making some of the most significant contributions to literature and literary studies in the Suisse romande.[7] Here let us consider briefly Corinna Bille and Alice Rivaz, two of Maillart's most cele-

brated contemporaries.[8] These women, unlike Maillart, wrote and remained close to home. Corinna Bille lived and wrote briefly in Paris
only to return to her native Valais. She gained fame not only for her
short stories—"La Demoiselle sauvage" (1974) won the prix Goncourt
for the *nouvelle*—but also for requesting a typewriter from her husband, fellow author Maurice Chappaz, immediately following the
birth of her second child. In her essays and novels, Alice Rivaz wrote
about the situation of working women in French-speaking Switzerland and never strayed far from home. She continued her office job so
that she might write on the side. These two women authors lived to
write and wrote what they lived. In the case of Cendrars and Bouvier,
they traveled in order to fuel their writing. Maillart fits neither of
these models well: she, in fact, wrote to travel. Like Alice Rivaz,
Maillart needed to work to support herself. She could count neither
on family money nor on a husband's indulgence. She wrote travel
books—very popular ones—to pay for her travels.

As such, Maillart hardly matches the model of the wealthy or
bourgeois Victorian woman traveling from England. The young Swiss
woman undoubtedly perceived the world somewhat differently than
many of the women who preceded her. How did her national identity
color and form her perception of self and the Other? Edward Said
suggests in his oft-cited *Orientalism* that the Orient is a European in-
vention, one that "existed as a set of values attached, not to its modern realities, but to a series of valorized contacts it had had with a
distant European past" (85). Clearly, Maillart belongs within the
scope of a European colonial analysis, but we can hardly locate her at
the center of this gaze. While Switzerland undoubtedly figures into
that European past, even Said acknowledges that Orientalism as a
discourse results primarily from a British and French cultural enterprise. Switzerland never established colonies of its own, preferring
instead to define national identity not through expansion but through
a rather precarious neutrality. This does not mean that Maillart did
not carry a certain colonial baggage with her, but rather, that her own
indoctrination into the colonial world differed from the understanding of her fellow French and British travelers. (This point becomes
particularly evident when she crosses China with the English Peter
Fleming, as I discuss later in chapter four.) Maillart did not have to
travel for the greater glory of England or France, for that burden was
never cast upon her.

Furthermore, because she traveled in the 1930s and 1940s, Maillart traveled at a time when the world began to question colonialism's unbridled expansion and practices. As Kowalewski observes: "Travel writers today often feel less culturally surefooted than their predecessors; correspondingly, the criticism that seeks to appraise the modern literature of travel must be both judicious and intellectually generous. It must be socially responsible without becoming solemn and prohibitive" (12). An analysis of Maillart's travelogues requires just this social responsibility because of her position on the brink of postcolonial criticism. She makes observations that express cultural awareness of her own presence as the Other/outsider. Because she does not fully belong to the colonial enterprise, she can perhaps better navigate around it in order to circumvent its imposed discourse.

Travel narratives and the difficulty of defining them undoubtedly contribute to Maillart's obscured status in the field of literary studies. Ranging from the Odyssey and the adventures of Marco Polo to the postmodern musings of Bruce Chatwin,[9] travel literature is particularly difficult to situate. As Kowalewski notes:

> Part of the reason this genre has been insufficiently recognized or studied piecemeal may have to do with its dauntingly heterogeneous character. Travel writing involves border crossings both literal and figurative...Travel writing borrows freely from the memoir, journalism, letters, guidebooks, confessional narrative, and, most important, fiction. (7)

Travel writing thus crosses disciplinary boundaries as well as literary ones. In her essay "Fieldwork in Common Places," Mary Louise Pratt comments on the inevitable affinity between travel writing and ethnography, noting that travel writing places narration first, description second, while ethnography reverses that order of emphasis (35). Travel writing undoubtedly owes its age-old popularity, at least in part, to its fluidity of form. This same fluidity makes travel writing difficult to classify as a particular literary genre or anthropological study. As Steve Clark explains in his introduction to *Travel Writing and Empire*: "The genre presents a problem for academic studies. It seems too dependent on an empirical rendition of contingent events, what happened to happen, for entry into the literary canon, yet too overtly rhetorical for disciplines such as anthropology, sociology, geography or history" (2).

The travel writer's cultural background and baggage further color this distinctly heterogeneous genre. Much has been written on English travel writing and the colonial enterprise. Said's *Orientalism* asserts that travel reinforced the Westerner's superiority, highlighting the division between the privileged, civilized occidental and the primitive, exotic other. Travelers from the West inevitably espoused the virtues of Orientalism and expansionism, "For Orientalism was ultimately a political vision of reality whose structure promoted the difference between the familiar (Europe, the West, "us") and the strange (the Orient, the East, "them")" (43). While Said's analysis applies to Europeans in general, it certainly speaks most directly to the large, colonial powers of England and France, where the colonial enterprise was central to national identity. For English and French travelers of the nineteenth and early twentieth centuries, travel writing helped travelers at home and abroad map out the roles of colonizer and colonized, powerful and powerless. While the echo of the colonial world undoubtedly influences Maillart's writing, it does not play an important role in her understanding of national identity. Furthermore, Maillart did not actually travel to the English or French colonial world until late in her career, when the outbreak of the Second World War prompted her to pursue a lengthy stay in India. Post-colonial theory thus provides a less than satisfactory way in which to read many of Maillart's texts. As Susan Morgan writes in *Place Matters*: "Postcolonial critics need to start seriously taking into account that not everybody was colonized and that this fact mattered a great deal both to them and to the British traveling in and writing about their states" (16). Maillart, unlike many of her contemporaries, writes in the margins of this colonial tradition about places that exist at the very edges of the colonial world.

How, then should we read Maillart's accounts of her travels to the ex-Soviet Union, China, and Afghanistan? Maillart inscribes her cultural understanding onto her snapshots of the world, constructing images of exotic other, through both photographs and narrative. The other takes form through her encounters with people and places little known in the West. The narration of adventure includes navigating the train stations of the remote corners of the Soviet Union and examining the people and places that lie before her. Maillart's travel books present revealing looks at women and men struggling to retain their way of life in a world of change. She sets her descriptions against the backdrop of unfamiliar landscapes and the simple but sometimes arduous task of continuing her travels. Her perspective is somewhat unusual because she does not travel as a government envoy or as a rich merchant's wife, but as a journalist or special correspondent seeking to tell the story of nomads and indigenous peoples. Her search for an elusive, lost way of life brings her face to face with her own misconceptions about others, Asia, and herself.

Maillart thus does not fit the mold of the colonial expatriate, but she does belong to a cohort of travel writers who gained fame between the two World Wars. Paul Fussell's well known *Abroad: British Traveling Between the Wars* might at first seem particularly unsatisfying for an analysis of Maillart, for Fussell limits himself to English travelers, and more specifically, to English men. Clearly, Maillart does not fit these parameters. Yet Maillart has a place in Fussell's historical rubric, one for which he has been strongly criticized. According to Fussell, the late 1930s represent the end of an era, the end of all serious travel writing: "The going was good for only twenty years, and after the war all that remained was jet tourism among the ruins" (226). While I would contend that the second half of the twentieth century saw travel writing flourish not fade,[10] I would certainly agree with Fussell that the early twentieth century saw travel literature at one of its most popular junctures. Maillart participated in and benefited from the lust for travel that prompted readers to buy books and travelers to write them. Indeed, the period was ripe for travel writing: the average citizen could not travel easily to the four corners of the globe but was eager to read about those who did. The absence of other media meant that people read about travels rather than learning about the world from television or movies. Moreover, during the 1920s and 1930s, the novel did not carry the prestige it does today. Its importance grew with the reputations of Joyce, Proust, Hemingway, and others during this same time frame. As Fussell notes, "Between the wars writing travel books was not at all considered incompatible with a serious literary career" (213). Maillart, Fleming, and others belonged to just such a vibrant literary community that has since faded with the passing of time.

Fussell's analysis has other strengths, including his discussion of Peter Fleming, Ella Maillart's traveling companion during their joint trek across China. His reading of Fleming creates a useful context in which to understand both Fleming and Maillart. In addition, Fussell's consideration of the role of the heroic quest in the travel book will prove helpful in mapping the strategies of Maillart's own texts. As Fussell writes, the travel narrative follows specific tropes that guide both author and reader:

> As in romance, the modern traveler leaves the familiar and predictable to wander, episodically, into the unfamiliar or unknown, encountering strange adventures, and finally, after travail and ordeals, returns safely. Somehow, we feel a travel book isn't wholly satisfying unless the traveler returns to his starting point: the action, as in a quest romance, must be completed. (208)

Maillart's texts, as we will see later on, follow this same episodic trajectory.

Fussell, like Said, disregards women travelers of the time, a choice that might lead the reader to think that few women even engaged in travel writing. Fussell's discussion, for example, of Freya Stark, a contemporary who corresponded periodically with Maillart, is remarkably short: "Someone is sure to ask why I've not dealt with the travel books of Freya Stark, and I will have to answer that to write a distinguished travel book you have to be equally interested in (1) the travel and (2) the writing. In Stark's works, admirable as the travel has been, the dimension of delight in language and disposition, in all the literary contrivances, isn't there" (197). Fussell thus rejects Freya Stark and simply ignores other British women who contributed to travel writing between the wars. For Fussell, women writers lack both literary merit and a true sense of adventure.

In reality, as Sara Mills points out in her work, *Discourses of Difference: An Analysis of Women's Travel Writing and Colonialism*, hundreds of British women traveled between 1850 and 1940 and they lacked neither literary sense nor an adventurous streak. I would add to that number the many women from other European countries who traveled the globe and wrote to tell of it, including Isabelle Eberhardt, Alexandra David-Néel, Annemarie Schwarzenbach, and of course, Ella Maillart. The choice to ignore women travel writers is perhaps not surprising considering the lot of women in the tradition of the travel narrative itself. As Karen Lawrence points out in her book, Penelope Voyages: "In the multiple paradigms of the journey plot— adventure, pilgrimage, exile, for example—women are generally excluded, their absence establishing the world of the journey as a realm in which the man confronts the 'foreign'" (1). To render the woman present, to re-inscribe her into the very tradition that she helped to forge, let us turn to some of the feminist theory on the travel narrative.

Mills locates her discussion of Foucault's work amidst competing discourses, namely colonial and feminist. She goes on to critique both Fussell and Said, referring to the long-standing tradition that essentially ignores women's travel narratives: "There is a tradition of reading women's writing as trivial or as marginal to the mainstream, and this is certainly the attitude to women's travel writing, which is portrayed as the records of the travels of eccentric and rather strange spinsters" (61). Mills also points to the failure of Orientalism when considering women's texts:

> The work of women travel writers cannot be fitted neatly within the Orientalist framework, and seems to constitute an alternative and undermining voice because of the conflicting discourses at work in their texts. They cannot be said to speak from outside colonial discourse, but their relation to the dominant discourse is problematic because of its conflict with the discourses of 'femininity,' which were operating on them in equal, and sometimes stronger, measure. (63)

Mills analysis thus brings women writers to center stage, but remains ethnocentric in its concentration on British writers. Even in her case study of Alexandra David-Néel, the one non-British writer she considers, Mills reduces David-Néel's European/ French identity to an English one, adding that David-Néel wrote *My Journey to Lhasa* in English. Only in a footnote to the text does Mills acknowledge that the book was originally written in French and later translated by the author into English. Likewise, Mills discusses Tibet as a British colony, never referring to the region's precarious position between British India, the Soviet Union, and China: her very British reading of geography and David-Néel's text fails to bring into question the author's position within this colonial discourse. Indeed, Mills' Foucauldian reading may at once be the strength and weakness of her analysis because she does not prescribe or explain how to read women's texts that fall outside of the dominant mode of discourse.

Maillart, like Alexandra David-Néel, wrote within the discourse of European colonialism, but if Britain and even France are at the heart of this matrix, Maillart and Switzerland inscribe themselves somewhere in the margins, away from the colonial center. Likewise, Maillart falls outside of the discourse of female domesticity: she never

married and traveled of her own accord. Finally, Maillart does not fit
the model of the aristocratic or bourgeois traveler: she had to earn her
living, and wrote and published in order to travel. In fact, Maillart fits
Mills' description of the exceptional individual cited earlier, the role
attributed to many women travelers in the early twentieth century. In
order to read Maillart's texts as more than those of the eccentric spinster, this analysis will seek to create the appropriate context for her
particular mode of discourse.

The appropriate context includes the voices of the men and
women who traveled with and at the time of Ella Maillart. Studies
like Fussell's give a lengthy account of British men, and several more
recent books by Lawrence, Mills, Morgan, and others chronicle the
writings of English travelers of the same period. Mary Kingsley's and
Isak Denison's accounts of life in Africa are also widely known. In
order to expand this field of discourse, we need not look far.
Alexandra David-Néel and Freya Stark might be logical starting
points because not only did they travel during the same interwar period, but they corresponded periodically with Maillart. Alexandra
David-Néel, a fellow French speaker and author of numerous texts on
her voyages to Tibet, China, and India, shared the same reading public as Maillart, and their letters indicate pangs of rivalry, if not jeal-
ousy, on both sides. Maillart and David-Néel on occasion translated
their own texts into English in an effort to increase their earning
power and readership.[11] Freya Stark, quickly dismissed by Fussell despite her renown and popularity at home and abroad, also corresponded with Maillart. Stark writes from her very British perspective
about her trips to the Middle East, including Syria and Iraq, countries
that did fall outside of British colonial rule. Annemarie
Schwarzenbach, Swiss German author, photographer, and poet, traveled across Afghanistan with Maillart on the eve of the Second World
War. Her correspondence with Maillart continues until
Schwarzenbach's premature death in 1942. Outside of Maillart's immediate circle of friends and acquaintances, women travelers at the
turn of the century helped pave the way for Maillart and her contemporaries. Isabelle Eberhardt's account of her life in Algeria, for example, provides some of the best known French travel letters of the period. In all of these cases, women reinvent the tropes of travel to cast
themselves as the protagonists. As Karen Lawrence points out:
"Women write the mythos of adventure and, more significant, trans-

form it. The gender of the viewer affects the ideology of the seeing as well as the tropes projected onto the foreign landscape" (17). How does Ella Maillart transform and adapt this mythos of adventure, this heroic quest? The pages that follow will trace the evolution of Maillart's travels from 1930 to 1940 in an effort to read toward a better understanding of both texts and contexts.

Ella Maillart originally had no intention of traveling to Asia, but when her plans to sail the South Pacific were foiled—best friend and sailing companion Miette de Saussure decided to get married rather than to pursue her sailing career—Maillart looked eastward. Her initial voyage to Russia in 1930 piqued her sense of adventure. The twenty-seven year old Maillart gratefully accepted fifty dollars from Jack London's wife in Berlin and made her way to Moscow. As she wrote to her father:

> Tout d'abord je suis folle de joie car j'arrive à réaliser un des rêves que je caresse depuis trois ans : passer un mois à Moscou. Cette fois la chose se présente sous de bons auspices et de la manière suivante : l'agence américaine pour laquelle j'ai écrit des articles...a un correspondant à Moscou depuis trois ans, pour les questions politiques et sérieuses ; mais il paraît qu'il n'a pas l'œil pour les articles pittoresques, sur la vie de tous les jours, les sports entre autres. (Ella Maillart, letter to her father, 2 May 1930)

> [First of all, I am thrilled because I will be able to make a dream come true, one that I have been nursing along for the last three years: to spend a month in Moscow. This time everything is above board and came about as follows: the American agency for which I write articles...has had a correspondent in Moscow for the last three years, someone responsible for political questions and other serious matters; but apparently he doesn't have an eye for more picturesque articles on everyday life, sports, and the like.]

Although Maillart traveled to Moscow to report on Russian cinema and youth sports, many assumed that Maillart entered the newly formed Soviet Union as a young communist. Maillart, for her part, never had any formal ties to the communist regime but saw no reason not to take advantage of the opportunity accorded her.[12] After a month in Moscow where she rowed with a local rowing team, Maillart managed to join a Soviet tourist youth excursion to the Caucasus. *Parmi la jeunesse russe* (1932) chronicles this singular outing, attesting to Maillart's sense of adventure as well as to her youthful naiveté. This is her first effort at a book-length manuscript and the pains of writing are fairly evident. Nonetheless, this travel book reveals points about Maillart and her perspective that are essential to the discussion of her work. *Parmi la jeunesse russe* serves as an initiation to writing and travel. Writing about the Caucasus, Maillart somewhat awkwardly reveals what will become the signature feature of her travel narratives: her telling looks at women, their work and lives. She observes, for example, the composition of society, the role of women, and the importance of family:

> Les femmes d'un certain âge ramènent toutes un coin de leur fichu non seulement sur leur menton comme les paysannes russes, mais jusque sur leur nez ; pourtant ici les femmes ne furent jamais voilées ou séquestrées. Au contraire, il existe même des traces de matriarcat dans le pays : lors des banquets rituels, la tamada, une femme coiffée d'un large chapeau, la doyenne de la famille, est major de table ; ses ordres sont ponctués de coups de pistolet tirés en l'air. (*Parmi la jeunesse russe* 144)

> [Women of a certain age all pull a corner of their scarf not only under their chin like the Russian peasants do, but right up to their nose; yet here these women have never been veiled or confined to separate quarters. On the contrary, there are even traces of matriarchy in this country: at ritual banquets, the tamada, a woman wearing a large hat, the senior member of the family, is the head of the table; her orders are punctuated by pistol shots into the air.]

Most noticeable, however, in this early report on Soviet leisure, is Maillart's surprisingly uncritical gaze. Although Maillart travels from the heart of capitalist Europe, her young idealism finds the communist initiative of sports for all workers inspiring. This same sense of idealism leaves her account mired in admiration for what the new government has achieved. Perhaps in reaction to a very positive account of the workings of the new Soviet republic, several reviews in the Swiss press accused Maillart of cavorting with communists. Nonetheless, the majority of critics in both Geneva and Paris responded favorably to Maillart's first literary venture. [13] With *Parmi la jeunesse russe*, the young Maillart sets the stage for future travels and future travel books.

Parmi la jeunesse russe thus serves as practical preparation for Maillart, who learns to negotiate the Soviet bureaucracy of permits, visas, and supplies. She also learns what her publisher and readers expect, and the trials and tribulations of her first book give way to a more assertive prose style in *Des Monts célestes aux sables rouges* (1934).

This second travel piece abandons any political pretensions, signaling a subtle shift in the discursive mode. Instead of focusing on the newest politics of the regions, Maillart begins to pay closer attention to the people and cultures she encounters. In this case, the discourse of Soviet colonialism collides with Maillart's non-Soviet perspective. Amidst these competing voices, Maillart begins to invent the image of the Other at the same time that she first considers the understanding and creation of self. The Other takes shape in the foreign landscapes and in the faces of the nomadic tribes and indigenous people who are just coming under Soviet rule. Maillart constructs the people and places she encounters through a combination of observation, story telling, history, and legend. What begin as more general observations move toward the specific as Maillart spends more time among the nomadic tribes. As she moves from the city into the shadows of the Tien Shan[14] mountains, Maillart is better able to study the communities of yurts that unfold before them. She recognizes that their very lifestyle is put into danger by the Soviet push toward collectivism: "Pour combien de temps leurs descendants (des nomades turco-mongols) vivront-ils encore comme il y a mille et dix mille ans? Maintenant que les bolcheviks cherchent à sédentariser, collectiviser (…)" (86). [For how much longer will their descendants go on living as they lived a thousand and ten thousand years ago? Now that the Bolsheviks are trying to settle them, collectivize them(…) (*Turkestan Solo* 72).] This recognition registers as an initial criticism of the Soviet colonial enterprise.

The Other thus takes shape in the faces of the nomadic tribes and indigenous people who are just coming under the control of the Soviet regime. They come to embody Maillart's own restlessness, offering an alternative to a more sedentary life in the west. Her definition of self forms in this same image, replacing the nomad's path with the traveler's ever changing itinerary. For the next ten years, Maillart will fit Bouvier's notion of the wandering Swiss living in a self-appointed exile.

By the time Maillart writes of her crossing of China with Peter Fleming in *Oasis interdites* (1937), the Other has assumed new forms. The Chinese, Mongolian, and Tibetan tribes fill the role of the wandering nomad, but Maillart confronts an equally foreign other in Fleming. Fleming's English nature coupled with his colonial and masculine understanding of China separate him from his traveling companion. Indeed, it is hardly surprising the Maillart and Fleming had never any intention of traveling together, but agreed to only when their journeys could not be realized separately. Nowhere is the colonial binarism that equates the male and the powerful colonizer, opposing them to the female other and colonized more readily apparent. Maillart's desire, and at some level her obligation, to identify with the people they encounter during the 3800 mile crossing distinguishes *Oasis interdites* from Fleming's *News from Tartary* (1936). In writing the second account of the same voyage, Maillart follows the twists and turns of travel writing described by Mills in *Discourses of Difference*: "The conventions of travel writing thus present a framework of largely masculine narratorial positions and descriptive patterns with which women writers negotiate when they construct their travel accounts" (86). The result is two travel books that present the same journey in two very different forms and perspectives.

The authorial gaze, the way in which Maillart sees and interprets the world, shifts from the Other to the self and back again in Maillart's *The Cruel Way* (1947), later translated by the author and published in French as *La Voie cruelle* (1952).[15] Maillart's story of the crossing of Afghanistan in the company of Annemarie Schwarzenbach appeared in the Virago series on women travelers in the United States in 1986. The female double, played by a thinly disguised Schwarzenbach and known to the reader as Christina, plunges into her morphine addiction and comes to represent a singular failure for the older Maillart: she can never rescue Schwarzenbach from her demons, and she will never save Afghanistan from the onslaught of the West. Her gaze, focused mainly on her friend's deteriorating condition, thus moves from the foreign Other to her traveling companion and then to herself. *The Cruel Way* marks a turning point in Maillart's literary career as she moves her focus from the outer to the inner voyage. Like *Oasis interdites*, *The Cruel Way* chronicles the rhythmic routine of daily life in Afghanistan while adding to it the joy of discovery. Indeed, Maillart seems at home amidst the landscapes and cultures of central Asia. She seeks to unmask the Afghani women behind their veil without much success. As Karen Lawrence writes: "Female oppression is itself complicated when the European white woman traveler confronts colonialism's other, sometimes another woman" (18). Cast as the oppressor and the oppressed, Maillart navigates the lonely road that leads to India, thus parting with Schwarzenbach and leaving behind a Europe in crisis.

While this analysis will focus specifically on Maillart's voyages during what Fussell refers to as the heyday of travel literature, the 1930s, it is certainly worth noting her other contributions to the genre. Her gaze turns inward when Maillart settles in India, the setting for *Ti-Puss* (1951), her writings on the five years she spent in the presence of the Indian sage Ramana Maharishi. Because *Ti-Puss* comes later and moves away from the genre of travel literature, I will discuss it briefly in the concluding chapter. Maillart's final book traces the lengthy journey of the soul, and ultimately, this image should move beyond the self that she has worked hard to invent. Maillart's gaze thus completes its shift from the outer to the inner journey: what begins in search of a certain exotic adventure ends in the pursuit of a spiritual understanding of people and place.[16]

By turning to the spiritual in British-occupied India, does Maillart ignore or overlook her relationship to the colonial world? Partly because she exists in the margins of this discourse, Maillart looks beyond the colonial hierarchy: she makes a conscious refusal to participate in a war created in Europe by the colonial powers and does not return to Switzerland. She abstains from all that the war implies, including resistance, in an effort to find an elusive inner peace for herself. What began as a search for the exotic evolves into the inner journey of the soul. As Mary Morris writes in her article "Women and Journeys: Inner and Outer": "Because of the way women have cultivated their inner lives, a journey often becomes a dialogue between the inner and the outer, between our emotional necessity and the reality of the external world" (30). Maillart's gaze no longer divides the self and Other, but looks for a unifying whole. In a way, Maillart's efforts are a final grasp for modernist wholeness in a world that is about to fall into post-modern turmoil. Her five years in India attest not to her movement toward the colonial model, but to her desire for a spiritual alternative to what she interprets as chaos in Western society. India thus becomes the civilized world, subverting, at least in Maillart's understanding, the colonial hierarchy.

Maillart returned to Switzerland in 1945 and spent most of the next fifty years in Geneva and the alpine village of Chandolin, where she died in her chalet in the spring of 1997. Her travelogues remain as a legacy to an Asia that has since been transformed by modernization and the post-colonial era. They allow for a brief glimpse at people and places with which the western world remains unfamiliar even today. The chapters that follow examine how Maillart presents and analyzes her observations and experiences. Chapter two, "Exile and the Traveler's Gaze," discusses the role of exile and expatriation in the traveler's understanding of the world. Chapter three, "From the Caucasus to the Tien Shan: Politics and Travel in the Soviet Republic," focuses on *Parmi la jeunesse russe* et *Des Monts célestes aux sables rouges* and the apprenticeship of the young writer. Chapter four, "Diverging Perspectives: Ella Maillart and Peter Fleming on China," is devoted to the stereoscopic vision that Maillart's *Oasis interdites* and Fleming's *News from Tartary* provide on their trek across China. Chapter five, "Driving in a Ford: Two Women Across Afghanistan," problematizes the transition from the outer to the inner journey and the relationship that develops between Maillart and Annemarie Schwarzenbach. Finally, the concluding chapter, "On Travel and Coming Home," includes a discussion of Maillart's texts written in India as well as excerpts from my interview with Ella Maillart in the summer of 1996 in order to articulate Maillart's transformed understanding of home and travel.

To conclude this introduction, let us consider Karen Lawrence's question, "can women writers revise the various plots of wandering (in romance, adventure, exploration, and travel narratives) without succumbing to the traditional pitfalls of these plots for a feminine protagonist?" (17). Maillart's own narrative journey sees her writing and rewriting the traveler's quest for discovery. Yet Maillart's writing offers more than a series of exploits completed by an exceptional in-dividual or an eccentric spinster. Maillart effectively transforms the travel book and deflects the colonial gaze, writing herself into the plot as she comes to terms with the foreign Other. Her travel writing pro-vides a fascinating look at the construction of the Other and the re-lated construction of self for a narrator and protagonist who functions outside of the dominant discourse. By weaving a context of her con-temporaries and reinserting the travel book into the center of the lit-erary scene, we can inscribe Ella Maillart into a long, rich tradition of women's travel writing.

Notes

1   In Switzerland, the group Les Amis d'Ella Maillart work to promote her works and memory. There is a small but lovely museum in the village of Chandolin devoted to Maillart's works and travels. While she remains a popular figure, little attention has been paid to her works at the university level.

2   See Fussell's *Abroad: British Traveling Between the Wars.*

3   Nicolas Bouvier (1929–1998) traveled throughout the world, living at some length in Japan, and voyaging across much of Asia. Like Maillart, he traveled through Afghanistan via car. He went to Maillart for advice prior to his departure in 1952, and Maillart told him "Partout où des hommes vivent, un voyageur peut vivre aussi..." (*La Vie immédiate* 7). They remained friends for life.

4   It is interesting to note that while Bouvier deliberately speaks of "la Suisse" in its feminine form, he addresses primarily male travelers and writers.

5   Unless otherwise noted, all translations are my own.

6   Cendrars once even offered Maillart lessons in prose because he did not consider her to be a real writer, but she was too busy traveling to accept his offer.

7   For an introduction to women writers in French-speaking Switzerland in the second-half of the twentieth century see *Solitude surpeuplée: Femmes écrivains suisses de langue française* and the introduction by Doris Jakubec.

8   S. Corinna Bille, born in 1919, died in 1979. Alice Rivaz, born in 1901, died a year after Ella Maillart, in 1998.

9   An Englishman who traveled extensively in Asia, Africa, and South America, Chatwin gained fame and praise for his travel books in the 1970s and 1980s by probing the relationship between place and "placelessness." He wrote seven travel novels before he died at the age of 48.

10 From Peter Mayle to Mary Morris, from the *Lonely Planet* to *Let's Go*, travel writing has grown and diversified in the late twentieth and the early twenty-first centuries. The genre reaches armchair travelers and intrepid trekkers alike. Fussell predicted that travel literature would die as soon as the masses could reach what had been considered the most unreachable places on earth. Instead, travel literature continues to evolve and transform itself.

11 When feasible, Maillart had her travel narratives translated by a translator. Such is the case for *Cruises and Caravans, Gypsy Afloat,* and *Ti-Puss.*

12 Maillart never speaks of any personal ties to the communist party in *Parmi la Jeunesse russe.* On her visa application, she is asked about the purpose of her trip to the Soviet Union " Quel est le but de votre séjour en URSS ? ...'Étudier les conditions du sport et du cinéma', deux questions qui m'intéressent particulièrement" (13).

13 For a more detailed discussion of the critical reception of *Parmi la jeunesse russe,* see chapter three.

14 The Tien Shan or Tian Shan mountains extend from the Pamirs in central Asia northeast into Sinkiang. They are known in French as *des Monts célestes* or the *T'ien Chan*.

15 Maillart wrote *The Cruel Way* while living in India. There she decided to write in English rather than French. I will cite the original versions of Maillart's texts throughout this book. As a result, quotations from *The Cruel Way* will appear in English while the texts that precede it will be cited in French.

16 Likewise, Maillart composed *Gypsy Afloat*, published in English in 1942, during her years in India. Because *Gypsy Afloat* chronicles her sailing experiences, its contents focus primarily on her activities in the mid-1920s. I will consider *Gypsy Afloat* briefly in the context of Maillart's stay in India in chapter six.

Chapter Two

Exile and the Traveler's Gaze

The traveler has, in some ways, committed herself to exile. While neither banished nor threatened by a specific political agenda, the traveler chooses to live away from home, from all that is familiar. The traveler's self-imposed exile equips her with an outsider's look at the places and people she encounters, for the traveler quite naturally understands new spaces in relation to the home she left behind. For many travelers in the first half of the twentieth century, this meant transplanting or transforming British customs and landscapes. Ella Maillart, for her part, gives voice to an emerging perspective, one that evolves outside of the British colonial dynasty but within the greater context of European imperialism. Historically, Maillart finds herself writing between two World Wars, events that obviously influenced her career and colored her gaze. Professionally, Maillart established her career as a journalist, photographer, and author, and thus brought three distinct perspectives to her traveling and writing. This second chapter will examine exile and the traveler's gaze in the context of Ella Maillart's life and writing. I will discuss, in particular, exile, expatriation, and their role in the creative process. This chapter will go on to explore how Maillart saw and understood foreign spaces and places, paying close attention to her historical and professional perspectives. Finally, this analysis will consider the end of exile and the significance of returning home. Following this trajectory will allow us to inscribe Maillart's career in the well-documented canon of travel writers who came of age in the 1920s and 1930s; furthermore, this analysis will allow us to better understand the images that Maillart brings back to us in her photos and travel books.

The traveler ventures into the world of exile and expatriatism, two terms that Edward Said defines in his essay "Reflections on Exile." Whereas exile connotes the negative, expatriatism carries more positive associations. As Said notes: "Exile originated in the age-old practice of banishment. Once banished, the exile lives an anomalous and miserable life, with the stigma of being an outsider" (362). This hardly provides an accurate definition for Maillart's situation, but it does align exile and the outsider. Said's definition of expatriate might better explain Maillart's voluntary exile: "Expatriates voluntarily live in an alien country, usually for personal or social reasons. Hemingway and Fitzgerald were not forced to live in France. Expatriates may share in the solitude and estrangement of exile, but they do not suffer under its rigid proscriptions" (362–3). Maillart's expatriatism allowed her to leave behind the constraints of home and even profit from the estrangement that expatriatism imposed. Solitude and estrangement bring her to writing.

Expatriatism is, however, experienced differently by men and women, as Shari Benstock aptly points out in her article "Expatriate Modernism: Writing on the Cultural Rim" (23). For Maillart, what began as a rite of passage—a young Swiss woman leaves home to work as a French teacher in an English school—turned into nearly a twenty year journey. Leaving home, Maillart encountered the freedom of movement and spirit that seemed to elude her in Switzerland. This experience proves to be consistent with that of other women writers and travelers. As Susan Stanford Friedman explains:

> Expatriatism provided freedom of mind and spirit. Freedom from what, we might ask. From convention, from the pressure to conform, to do the respectable, the proper, the expected. For women, the pressure to conform centered on the question of gender. Freedom of mind and spirit meant above all freedom from family pressure to conform to conventional norms. ("Exile in the American Grain: H.D.'s Diaspora" 94–5)

Such was the case for Ella Maillart. Options in Geneva included secretarial work and marriage, neither of which interested the young adventurer. As Maillart notes in her autobiography *Cruises and Caravans*:

> My position was difficult and was to remain so for many years. I was rejecting my father's advice to 'build up your life on material security.' Security, situation, consideration meant little to me. Like those other words, 'family,' 'religion,' they sounded empty: because the deep reality they stood for was fading away they were propped up with all sorts of explanations. I was going to look for something else. (24)

Maillart's self-imposed exile freed her from the societal constraints projected by her father. Her travels and travel writing thus become a realization of the freedom that exile may offer.

Maillart's first adventures away from the shores of Lake Geneva involved sailing. She chose to teach in a small school in Wales because of its proximity to the sea. Sailing, a lifelong passion, united her love for the outdoors and for the unconventional. Life on a boat suited Maillart's sense of adventure. Before hiring herself out as a cook and a first mate, Maillart had already established a record as an accomplished sailor. She had skippered an all female crew from southern France to Greece and competed for Switzerland in sailing in the 1924 Olympics. Sailing did more, however, than feed her sense of adventure. Sailing also nourished her budding political consciousness. Maillart sailed to leave behind a Europe bent on self-destruction. She harbored the same dreams as her hero and fellow sailor, Alain Gerbault.[1] Like Gerbault, Maillart dreamed of abandoning the crumbling European civilization in favor of an idyllic South Pacific:

> Our hearts had been nursing similar dreams: to reach the paradise of the South Seas! But Alain Gerbault...was on the eve of departure. As an air-pilot in the World War, with three companions he had decided to sail to the Pacific, to leave for ever a continent where such wars were possible. (*Cruises and Caravans* 22)

Gerbault, died in 1941 in East Timor after spending the last nine years of his life in the South Pacific; Maillart, after sailing with several crews on the North Atlantic, abandoned the sea in favor of travel across Asia. She retained, however, her pacifist dream and longing for an alternative to a Europe intent on war.

Once she has lived away from Geneva, Maillart recognizes that, for the moment, nothing compels her to return home. As Judith Kegan Gardiner explains in her essay "The Exhilaration of Exile:" "Thus exile must be defined in terms of time as well as place. We know that we can't go home again, that childhood memories and families of our youth no longer exist" (143). Indeed, no longer able to return to childhood delights on Lake Geneva, unwilling or perhaps unable to confront the expectations that await her at home, Maillart turned her attention to the east. She traveled first to Germany to work as a stunt person and movie double, then onto Moscow and the vast expanses of Russia. Her first trip to Russia inspired a series of future voyages that would take Maillart across Asia and back again: from the Caucasus to central Asia, from Peking to the Himalayas, from Sofia to Afghanistan, from Kabul to southern India. From 1930–1945 Maillart crisscrossed Asia on foot, on horseback, by ski, by truck, and by train. She actively sought the peaceful well being that she associated with the nomadic, even primitive lifestyles she encountered. Asia replaced Maillart's dream of the South Pacific.

Maillart recorded her observations in her photographs and travel books, creating images of other places and other faces so different from what she associated with home. Elsewhere thus becomes the context from which Maillart chooses to write. As Jane Marcus notes in her article "Alibis and Legends: The Ethics of Elsewhereness, Gender, and Estrangement:"

> For elsewhere is not nowhere. It is a political place where the displaced are always seen and see themselves in relation to the "placed". Dis/placement and difference as categories of political and gender exile from writing, speaking, and acting circulate around notions of fixed positions in a substantial Somewhere. (270)

In Maillart's case, exile is a political choice that displaces her from the brewing conflict in Western Europe. Expatriatism confirms her willingness to share in alternative political ideologies—she eagerly travels to the newly formed Soviet Union to participate in the government-run youth programs—and highlights her refusal to live within the confines of Swiss, bourgeois society. Her exile from conformism sparks her creative work.

Maillart's exile effectively inspired her writing and observations. Clearly, Maillart's observations are informed by the world she that has chosen to leave behind. At the same time, as a travel writer rather than an anthropologist or an ethnographer, Maillart did not need to isolate her subjects as objects to be studied. In his article, "Le voyage ethnologique,"[2] Pascal Dibie explains that "Le voyageur est celui dont l'œil ne cadre pas encore avec ce qu'il réfléchit, l'ethnologue celui qui réfléchit dans un cadre et, comme pour les mettre d'accord, l'écrivain serait celui qui voyage hors cadre avec ses mots sur le terrain de l'ethnologue. Tout cela pour dire que les voyageurs n'échappent pas à l'ethnologie, ni les ethnologues au voyage" (56). [The traveler is one whose eye does not yet frame things according to what he thinks, while the ethnologist is one who thinks within a framework and, as if to bring them together, the writer would be one who travels outside of this framework with his or her words embedded in ethnology. All this to say that neither the traveler escapes ethnography, nor the ethnographer travel.] As such, Maillart's interpretation of the world she encounters becomes a product of her very particular and undoubtedly subjective gaze. Her gender allowed her to make observations about women and children that may not have appeared subject-worthy to her male counterparts. Her lack of finances even permitted her to view things that others might have missed. As Maillart explained during a 1952 radio interview in England:

> So, I am very grateful that I have been poor because it obliged me to travel in a different way from other travellers, or journalists, or explorers. When they have a sort of self-contained unit and they have all their cooks and their tins and their boxes, they don't get in touch with the people of the country so much—they probably miss something. I couldn't speak the languages of all these nomads and Mongols and Tibetans, but because you try to live as they live and you are in the tent with them and so on, you're forced to imbibe something of their ways and thoughts and reactions. ("Woman's Hour : Ella Maillart")

Elsewhere thus becomes somewhere in Maillart's narrative, a somewhere where she lives with and among the people indigenous to the various stops in her journey. This somewhere does not qualify as home, but these ever-changing points on the map of Asia become the heart of her travel narratives.

Maillart understood Asia to be an alternative to a Europe that held no hope; she brought with her the disillusionment that characterized so many young Europeans after the Great War. Traveling in the aftermath of the First World War and on the eve of the Second marked Maillart's conscience and informed her gaze. In search of an elusive peace that may come with the simple lifestyle of the tribes of central Asia, Maillart embarked on her travels among the nomads of these little-known regions. As she notes in *Cruises and Caravans*:

> Except when I was sailing or skiing I felt lost, half alive. Everything I saw
> or read was depressing. The 'war to end war' was bringing in its train
> compromise, artificial ideals, and palavers that filed to establish a real
> peace. Growing uneasiness and lack of security seemed to confirm what
> Spengler had called the 'Decline of the West.' (28–9).

Maillart departed for Russia and later for central Asia in search of a
more successful paradigm for peaceful living. In fact, Asia became the
destination of nearly all of her future travels. Maillart traveled briefly
to Central America and North Africa during her life, but her main
focus remained elsewhere. Indeed, in search of spiritual renewal,
Maillart journeyed across the Asian continent.

If Maillart's gaze was shaped historically by the two wars, geo-
graphically Maillart looked to the mountains to recreate visions of
home. Leaving the ocean behind her, Maillart's treks took her to the
Caucasus, to the mountains of Turkistan, to the high plateaus of
western China, and to the Himalayas. Mountains mark the Swiss
landscape with which she is so familiar; likewise mountains delimit
the Asian landscapes that Maillart later adopted as her own.
Mountains evoke the freedom and well being that Maillart associated
with her amateur skiing career and her youth. At the same time,
mountains function as borders, dividing countries, ideologies, people.
To climb to the top of a particularly formidable summit might be
equated with conquest, especially in the eyes of a male traveler.
Tamara Whited notes in her essay "The Mountain in Twentieth-
Century French Literature" that "the mountain is a supreme
challenge… a landscape no less privileged for being continually
"conquered" by the young alpinists" (203). The preeminence of the
relationship between man and mountain dominates some of
Switzerland's most well-known prose and is especially prominent in
the novels of Charles-Ferdinand Ramuz, Maillart's most celebrated
literary compatriot in the twentieth century. Ramuz emphasizes the
power and the unknown that characterize mountain living, paying
special attention to the effect of man's intrusion on the mountain in
novels like *La Grande peur dans la montagne* (1925) and *Derborence*
(1934).

Maillart, for her part, continually returns to the mountain and the
associated landscape for inspiration in her travel narratives. However,
her own use of imagery differs from these male models in two ways:

first, the female version of the mountain summit does not balance upon conquest. This is also consistent with Swiss woman writer S. Corinna Bille. Bille's many short stories including "La Fraise noire" and "La demoiselle sauvage", set in the mountains in the Valais, reconfigure our understanding of the mountain. The mountain does not represent conquest, but rather becomes a place that brings into question the surreal and the supernatural. Reality becomes distorted if not unrecognizable in several of Bille's short stories. Because she writes travel books rather than fiction, Maillart has no need to displace or subvert mountain symbolism. As with her compatriots, mountains do, however, shape Maillart's gaze, and in her case, open the door to other worlds. As she writes in *Des Monts célestes aux sables rouges*:

> Encore quatre cent mètres de neige profonde à brasser: nous sommes au col, arête semée de cailloux sur lesquels nous nous asseyons...Voici à mes pieds l'un des buts que je m'étais proposés: les montagnes chinoises habités par les Khirgises, le Sin-Kiang bouleversé par des courants opposés...Quelle joie ce serait de descendre là, de couper les ponts derrière soi, marche grisante vers l'inconnu aux mille visages. (*Des Monts célestes aux sables rouges* 133–4)

> [Still a quarter mile of deep snow to battle with: then we are at the pass, a rock strewn ridge, where we sit down...Here at my feet is one of the objectives I had set myself in coming so far: the Chinese mountains inhabited by Kirghiz, and Sin Kiang in the turmoil of opposing currents...What joy it would be to go down there and burn my boats behind me, and go on always, intoxicated by the Unknown's thousand faces! (*Turkestan Solo* 114–15)]

At the mountain pass, Maillart looks beyond having achieved one of her proposed goals to the vistas that rise before her. The mountain thus becomes a gateway to further travels and new understanding rather than yet another conquest.

At the same time, mountains inspire reflection for the traveler and individual. As Maillart writes in *Oasis interdites*:

> Puis je continue jusqu'au sommet rocheux qui s'élève au-dessus d'une région schisteuse sans végétation. Là-haut le vent règne: je suis à la hauteur de crêtes nombreuses et dénudées... Involontairement, je fais un retour sur moi-même. Depuis six mois, j'ai souvent eu l'impression de me trouver sur une planète différente, et je suis, à vrai dire, comme rayée déjà du reste du monde; ma famille, mes amis ont appris à se passer de moi;

mon éloignement, mon isolement m'ont enseigné enfin que je suis inutile à "l'ordre des choses"! (210)

[I went on to the rocky summit that towered over a slaty region where nothing grew. At the top the wind was strong. I was on a level with numerous bare crests...Unconsciously I grew introspective. During the last six months I had often had the impression of being on another planet. In fact, I was as though I had been shut off from the rest of the world. My family and friends had learned to do without me. My remoteness and isolation had at last taught me that I was useless to "the order of things." (*Forbidden Journey* 268)]

The thoughts born of these mountain vistas help Maillart make the transition from the outer to the inner journey. If indeed, as she suggests, her family and friends have learned to live without her, she may be without her own place in the world. The traveler lives a very particular experience of place and space: always far from home, the traveler must define and redefine her notion of self in relation to her new surroundings. The mountainous landscape allows Maillart to situate herself at once amidst the familiar and the foreign, recalling home while at the same time opening doors to new views, both literal and metaphoric.

The mountains' symbolic value is transformed when Maillart chooses to end her exile in 1945. At the end of World War II, Maillart returns home to Switzerland. For much of the year, she takes up residence in Chandolin. Situated at 2000 meters with a view of the Matterhorn, Chandolin recalls the mountain vistas of central Asia. Mountain peaks literally surround her small chalet, Atchala, named for the sacred summit overlooking the ashram she left behind in southern India.[3] Mountains separate heaven from earth, creating a new set of boundaries for the traveler who has returned from abroad.

Maillart's view of these mountains, her gaze onto the borders of the infinite, often came throughout the lens of her Leica camera. Her dual or even triple identity, that of photographer, journalist, and author, defined her gaze. Through her photographs, Maillart created her first images of self and other. As Roland Barthes explains in *La Chambre claire* "Car la Photographie, c'est l'avènement de moi-même comme autre: une dissociation retorse de la conscience d'identité" (28). [Because photography is the advent of myself as other: a twisted dissociation of identity consciousness.] Photography may indeed be Maillart's gateway into identity politics, bringing with it questions of subject/object, self/other, colonizer/colonized. Whom did Maillart photograph? To what end? For what audience? The answers to these questions will help us to understand better Maillart's traveler's gaze and her particular point of view.

Photography puts Maillart in a position of power over her subjects. She decides what to include in the lens's frame. At the same time, photography links the exotic to the mundane, connecting the world of the nomadic Asian tribe to the readers of the Royal Geographic Society's publications. As Susan Sontag notes in her essay "On Photography:"

> The photographer is supertourist, an extension of the anthropologist, visiting natives and bringing back news of their exotic doings and strange gear. The photographer is always trying to colonize new experiences or find new ways to look at familiar subjects—to fight against boredom. For boredom is just the reverse side of fascination: both depend on being outside rather than inside a situation, and one leads to the other. (42)

In fact, Maillart's camera serves as a reminder of the constant intrusion of the colonial world on the more remote corners of Asia. In Maillart's efforts to record and understand the peoples and cultures of central Asia, she cannot help but impose the photographer's dilemma as explained by Sontag: "Even the most compassionate photojournalism is under pressure to satisfy simultaneously two sorts of expectations, those arising from our largely surrealist way of looking at all photographs, and those created by our belief that some photographs give real and important information to the world" (105). Maillart seeks to balance the artistic and informational reception of her photos. Her photographs are informed by her experience as a traveler as well as by her editors', and by extension the readers', wishes. As a result, her photos mediate between these two poles.

Maillart's collection of photographs includes some 17,000 negatives housed today at the Musée de l'Elysée in Lausanne, Switzerland. The many rolls of film recorded landscapes, people, and everyday life. Most remarkable is Maillart's view of women, families, and her recording of daily activities. As noted earlier, Maillart photographed scenes that many of her colleagues would not have thought subject-worthy. Such is the case for several of the photos taken during her trek to the frontiers of Russian Turkistan, for example. One photo, entitled "The young Uzbek of Samarkand," shows an Uzbek boy, approximately fifteen years old, looking confidently into the camera.

He wears a large fur hat and several layers of coats as he awaits knives he brought for sharpening. He is adequately dressed, neither very rich nor very poor, and takes part in the bustling activity of the Samarkand marketplace (*La Vie immediate* 47). The second photo, "Samarkand," shows two young women finishing their photo session with the street photographer. One, visibly pregnant, raises her head-covering to reveal her round face and piercing stare. The second, dressed in a more western costume topped with an overcoat and a small head cap, prepares to pay the photographer (*La Vie immediate* 46). Both photos attest to the to the daily activity of the market, normalcy of their actions in what we would consider a very remote part of the world. They also mark the perhaps inevitable move from the traditional dress and lifestyle. Western influence cannot be avoided whether it comes in the guise of clothing or through a camera shutter. Maillart's camera and her prose give a brief glimpse of the Uzbecki boy and young women, giving them a place, if not a voice, in her travel book.

Photographs do not only tell the story of those portrayed. Maillart's images of young Tangoute women, photographed during her trek across China in 1935, attest to Maillart's presence as an outsider, to the intrusion of the camera. Frightened, or at least apprehensive, the girls gaze warily at the lens. Aware of their discomfort, Maillart records the following caption: "Effarouchées, deux jeunes filles tangoutes aux cent-huit tresses, aux manches raides traînant à terre, ne le laissent pas amadouer par mes sourires(…)" (*La vie immediate* 102). [Frightened, two young Tangoute girls with one hundred and eight braids, long, stiff sleeves reaching the ground, will not let themselves be mollified by my smiles.]The photographer's gaze assures her position as an outsider looking in, as a white woman who has no role in the indigenous society. Her outsider's status is reaffirmed by those she photographs, women whose eyes, in this case, reveal an unspoken distrust. The return gaze reveals thus as much about the photographer as about those photographed.

This fascination with the other, both women and men, helps Maillart to situate herself in a world where she is still looking to find her place, as her photographs remind us. As Sontag writes

> Photography is the paradigm of an inherently equivocal connection between self and world—its version of the ideology of realism sometimes dictating an effacement of the self in relation to the world, sometimes

authorizing an aggressive relation to the world which celebrates the self. One side or the other of the connection is always being rediscovered and championed. (123)

Maillart subordinates her own self to those pictured in her photographs. She is neither the heroine of her own narrative nor the savior of those whom she photographs. Photography brings her vision of the other to the forefront. This is especially true in her early narratives, *Parmi la jeunesse russe* and *Des Monts célestes aux sables rouges*, where the search for the other dominates the search for self. At the same time, Maillart always remains close by, Leica camera in hand. The operator of the camera has the final word on the image produced. She never travels without her Leica, reminding the reader that the reality presented by a snapshot depends upon the subjectivity of her gaze.

Photographs thus trace Maillart's voyages for the reader and present an evolution of sorts in her quest for peace and understanding. The photos from *Ti-Puss*, her travel book written after her five year stay in India, document the shift in the photographer's gaze. Her photographs of the Maharishi (Ti-Puss 49) and friend and poet Lewis Thompson (Ti-Puss 81), for instance, focus on the subjects' eyes: their outward gaze seems to attest to the importance of the inward one. The photos thus mirror Maillart's own transformation, one that leads from travel as such to an equally rigorous inner journey.

Photography thus helps define Maillart's relationship to the world and people around her. At one level, photography may help define Maillart as a European colonial, one who appropriates her photographic subject as one might buy a souvenir from a roadside attraction. As Sontag explains:

> Photography is acquisition in several forms. In its simplest form, we have in a photograph surrogate possession of a cherished person or thing, a possession which gives photographs some of the character of unique objects. Through photographs, we also have a consumer's relation to events, both to events which are part of our experience and to those which are not—a distinction between types of experience that such habit-forming consumership blurs. (155–6)

Maillart no doubt participates in this habit-forming type of consumerism. At the same time, Maillart's photos give faces to individuals who otherwise appear as unknown names on a foreign map.

If Maillart does indeed appropriate her subjects, it may be in an effort to write of herself. While this process may underline the narcissistic nature of photography, it also points to an awareness attained through the photographer's gaze. Photography allows Maillart to situate others at home; she recognizes herself as a traveler passing through, as one who creates meaningful ties to the places and people along the way through her collection of photographed memories.

Photography will go on to feed and encourage Maillart's other professional aspirations, specifically those of journalist and author. As a journalist, Maillart wrote articles to accompany the photographs she took. She often used her photos in guise of notes. Later this same process informed her literary career, one that began innocently enough. Shortly after having returned from her trip to the Caucasus, Maillart again sought out her friend Alain Gerbault in Paris. Gerbault had just finished his solo sail across the Atlantic and enjoyed celebrity status in France at the time. He introduced Maillart to his publisher Charles Fasquelle, as Maillart recounts in *Cruises and Caravans*:

> The publisher asked : 'Are you going to write something about your stay there ?' 'Oh, no!' I replied, 'I cannot write.'
> This answer impressed him so favourably—for nowadays every one with a fountain pen thinks he can write—that he insisted and asked me many questions. Suddenly I remembered my effort at writing in English and timidly mentioned it. At once he asked to see an expanded version in French. (50)

Fasquelle offered Maillart an advance of 6000 francs, more money than she had ever seen, and thus began her pattern of writing to travel.

This established pattern will continue for Maillart throughout the 1930s. Her need or desire to travel feeds, in turn, her authorial contracts and vice versa; for if the traveler may be forced to write in order to earn a living, the writer of travel narratives must venture far afield in order to assure the authenticity of her narratives. In his short article "Sur les traces des écrivains voyageurs," Jean Marie Goulemat notes

> Car c'est un paradoxe : en même temps qu'on accord une importance au style, à la singularité du regard et de l'écriture, à la différence de l'écrivain, on se croit obligé de donner les preuves matérielles de son départ et de son éloignement. Il ne s'agit plus simplement de faire vrai, il faut avoir vécu,

vu ce que l'on raconte. Voilà bien une raison supplémentaire de trouver nos voyageurs étonnants. (25)

[Because it is a paradox: at the same time we lend such importance to style, to the distinctive character of the gaze and the writing, to the author's sense of difference, we feel obliged to give material proof of one's departure and the distance traveled. It is no longer a question of simply making something seem real: we must have lived it, seen what we tell. Hence, just one more reason to find our travelers remarkable.]

In Maillart's case, throughout the 1930s the desire to travel seems to dominate her entire being, not unlike her fellow travel writers then and now, as Marc Kravetz points out:

"Ce qui semble en effet le lot de nos travel writers, écrivains voyageurs ou voyageurs qui écrivent, comme on voudra, mais d'abord habités par ce désir d'ailleurs, ils ne voyagent pas seulement pour trouver matière à écrire, mais à l'évidence ils obéissent à une pulsion plus forte qu'eux". ("L'alternative nomade" 63)

[That which seems, in fact, to be the lot of our travel writers, writers who travel or travelers who write, whichever you prefer, is that they are first and foremost consumed by this desire of elsewhere. They do not travel just to find writing material, but seem to obey an impulse stronger than themselves.]

As Kravetz describes, Maillart cannot resist the impulse to travel, and her career as a travel writer takes off after her contract with Fasquelle is confirmed. For the next fifteen years, she never looks back.

Maillart wrote *Parmi la jeunesse russe*, her first book, shortly after her return from the Soviet Union and prepared her trip to Russian Turkistan. She traveled equipped with her Leica as well as a small agenda. Her agenda notes would later serve as the basis for articles and her forthcoming travel book *Des Monts célestes aux sables rouges*. She took photos constantly and the developed films became yet another source for her prose. From her journalistic notes and a rich collection of negatives, Maillart began composing her collection of travel narratives. She crossed China in 1935 with her typewriter in tow, sending journal articles ahead when possible. This trip resulted in the publication of *Oasis interdites*. When she drove across Iran and Afghanistan in 1939 with Annemarie Schwarzenbach, the two women brought not only cameras and typewriters, but also the equipment needed for the making of a cinematographic film entitled *Nomades afghans*.[4] The use of film as medium further informed Maillart's gaze, offering yet another interpretation of the Other, space, and time. Several years later, Maillart wrote *The Cruel Way*, recording their adventures and somewhat tumultuous relationship in prose.

Travel and expatriation, photographic and filmed images, thus provided the impetus for Maillart to write. Away from home, she found not only the desire but also the need to write to support herself. Writing became at once a creative force and a necessity. Yet writing in French became nearly impossible after so much time spent in places where other languages are spoken. In fact, after five years in India, Maillart found herself in linguistic limbo: she began writing in English. For one thing, she acknowledged that she was less sensitive to grammatical errors and breaches of style when writing in English. In addition, those willing to read and correct her manuscript while she lived in India spoke and wrote in English. Finally, writing in English saved time and the added fee of hiring a translator. As a result, English became a sort of lingua franca for Maillart. *The Cruel Way, Ti-Puss, Gypsy Afloat*, and her autobiography *Cruises and Caravans* were all originally written in English, unlike her first three travel narratives written in French. Writing thus becomes part of her alienation and expatriation. Through the act of writing in English, Maillart distances herself from her life in French-speaking Switzerland, from her mother tongue, from her home. By the time Maillart returns from abroad in 1945, she has already distanced herself linguistically and psychologically from her Swiss origins. The expatriation thus functions on two levels: Maillart leaves behind both country and language. As a result, she creates an added distance between herself and her writing, between her earlier and later texts. Susan Hardy Aiken describes a similar process in the prose of Isak Dinesen who, like Maillart, earned her living, at least in part, by writing travel books:

> Beginning in geographical alienation, displacement operates in Dinesen's writing at many levels. Consider, for example, her extraordinary double textual system, her practice of writing virtually every text twice—once in English, as Isak Dinesen, then in Danish, as Karen Blixen…By choosing English as her primary literary language, she displaced herself from her native tongue; by rewriting the texts in Danish, she displaced them from their own ostensible origin(al)s" (115).

A similar analysis might be applied to Maillart's own texts. In fact, the split in Maillart's publications, the transition from French to English, also marks the move from the outer to the inner journey. The quest for other is later displaced by her search for self and the desire to transcend the self. The transition itself is most evident with the publication of *The Cruel Way*.[5] The five years Maillart spends in India en route to spiritual enrichment also bear witness to this transformation. By the time Maillart does go home to Switzerland, she is willing to exchange a life of wandering for one largely filled with contemplation.

In conclusion, let us return with Maillart from her self-imposed exile in 1945. Once Maillart reestablished herself in Switzerland, her literary career drew to a close. In order to provide for her mother, she relocated to Geneva for the winter months, but abandoned the city in favor of her mountain retreat for the rest of the year. Maillart published Ti-Puss in 1951, but then devoted her time to giving lectures and writing journal articles in order to earn her living. Maillart spent the next fifty years on other trajectories, traveling between Geneva and Chandolin and making regular trips to India and Nepal as a guide for tourists. She spent much of those years thinking and discussing, refining her understanding of eastern philosophies and spiritualism. When she turned 93 in 1996, Maillart decided to remain in Chandolin, the village situated at 2000 meters that reminded her of the mountain vistas of central Asia. There, where the clouds dart in and out from among the mountain peaks, Maillart spent the final year of her life. Perhaps Chandolin had finally become home.

Notes

1. Alain Gerbault had gained world-wide fame for his sailing exploits and financial support for his expeditions by the time he and Maillart met in 1922.

2. Dibie's article appears in the June 2004 *Magazine Littéraire*, an issue devoted to the subject of *les écrivains voyageurs*. In this special issue, Ella Maillart is one of seven travel writers noted in the section on twentieth-century travelers.

3. As noted in the chronology that follows Maillart's collection of letters to her mother, *Cette réalité que j'ai pourchassée*: "Conquise par la beauté et le silence de ce village perché à 2000 m dans les Alpes suisses, elle y construit en 1948 son chalet *Atchala*, en mémoire d'Arunatchala, colline sacrée dominant l'ashram de Ramana Maharishi" (168). [Subdued by the beauty and the silence of this village perched at 2000m in the Swiss alps, in 1948 she built her chalet Atchala there, in memory of Arunatchala, the sacred peak that dominated Ramana Maharishi's ashram.]

4. *Nomades afghans* was produced in 1940 at the conclusion of the trip through Afghanistan. The black and white, silent documentary by Ella Maillart and Annemarie Schwarzenbach lasts for 60 minutes. The film has been featured in various film festivals recently, especially as the world pays more attention to Afghanistan. In 2005, for example, *Nomades afghans* figured in a film series dedicated to travel writers at the Centre Pompidou in Paris.

5. The fifth and sixth chapters of this study discuss at some length the transition toward the inner journey and the desire to transcend the self in the context of *The Cruel Way* and subsequent texts.

Chapter Three

From the Caucasus to the Tien Shan: Politics and Travel in the Soviet Republics

Ella Maillart engages in a specific political agenda early in her career that will pave the way for all of her future travel books. As a young woman traveling to the newly formed Soviet Union, Maillart chooses the politics of anti-politics, literally rejecting political affiliation in favor of cultural observations. Her position is undoubtedly naive: is there an anti-political stance in a very politicized world? Perhaps not. But even so, by trying to remain politically neutral, Maillart opens doors for herself that remain closed to others. At the same time, she replicates, in effect, the neutrality espoused by her native Switzerland. This anti-political position obliges Maillart to consider and reconsider the colonial experience. She views first-hand the effects of Soviet colonial rule and evaluates the questionable, western notion of progress. This process brings Maillart to pay particularly close attention to the Other, to the people bearing the brunt of the Soviet colonial movement. Maillart is hardly a mouthpiece of criticism for Soviet collectivism. Nonetheless, her observations of the Other originate in her first trip across the Caucasus and become a dominant theme in future narratives. Indeed, in her move away from the overtly political, Maillart gives voice to those who cannot speak out against the colonial enterprise. Her anti-political discourse thus gives voice to the disenfranchised. Telling the story of the Other along with her observations of woman and daily life mark Maillart's travel books and focus her particular gaze. At the same time, *Parmi la jeunesse russe* and *Des Monts célestes aux sables rouges* document the trials and tribulations of establishing narrative voice. In the process, they set the stage for Maillart's particular brand of anti-politics, one that eventually leads to her refutation of war in Europe and the search for peace in India.

Parmi la jeunesse russe, published by Charles Fasquelle in 1932, represents Maillart's first literary endeavor, telling the story of her travels to Moscow and the Caucasus. The emphasis rests on Maillart's experience in Moscow and later outside of the Soviet capital. Little attention is paid to Maillart's entry into the Soviet Union. She discusses her visa request in the short foreword to her first book:

> Le lendemain, le goût du risque en moi, j'allai au consulat de l'Union des Républiques socialistes et soviétiques remplir ma demande de visa. Le questionnaire demandait : "Quel est le but de votre séjour en URSS?" ...aussi répondis-je : "Etudier les conditions du sport et du cinéma", deux questions qui m'intéressent particulièrement. Le consul était grand amateur des films; il m'en parla longuement et m'assura que l'on sera partout enchanté de répondre à ma curiosité. (13)

> [The next day, I felt like taking my chances and went to the consulate of the Union of Soviet and Socialist Republics to fill out my request for a visa. The questionnaire asked: "What do you intend to accomplish during your travels to the USSR?"...and so I replied: "I plan to study sport and cinema", two subjects that were of particular interest to me. The consul was a big film buff; he spoke to me at length and assured me that everywhere people would be delighted to satisfy my curiosity.]

Maillart reveals her interests in sport and cinema, but no mention is made of political party affiliation. In reality, at the time, many young communists did not actually belong to the official party. Maillart neither mentions her political affiliation, nor does she speak publicly about her political beliefs concerning communism or neutrality. As Michel Tatu notes in his preface to the 1989 printing of *Parmi la jeunesse russe*:

> Mais Ella Maillart se soucie d'autant moins de politique qu'elle évite, comme elle l'écrit, les " discussions d'ordre général" et n'a engagé aucun interprète. Ajoutons que c'était là une condition du voyage : toute question se rapportant "au gouvernement" aurait entraîné son expulsion immédiate, l'avait-on avertie. Sans parler du fait que toute information critique publiée aurait pu mettre en danger ses contacts à Moscou. (9)

> [But Ella Maillart worries little about politics and tries to avoid, as she writes, "discussions of the general order" and does not employ an inter-

preter. We should add that this was one of the conditions of her trip: any questions relating to "the government" would have resulted in her immediate expulsion, as she had been warned. It goes without saying that any information she published criticizing the regime would have put her contacts in Moscow in danger.]

By assuming what she interprets to be a politically neutral stance, Maillart neither condones nor condemns the communist regime. As Tatu indicates, her lack of engagement in politics and political discussion permits her to travel in the Soviet Union.

This does not imply that Maillart traveled without any political opinion. Clearly, the young traveler embraces many of the changes being imposed by the new regime. At the same time, she does not participate in or follow communist party politics, unlike many of the intellectuals who later travel to the Soviet Union. For her part, Maillart offers a unique look at Moscow in the 1930s, as Tatu points out in his preface:

Mais le présent récit a un autre avantage : celui d'allier la fraîcheur du reportage "sur le vif" à la nouveauté très particulière du sujet. Que savait-on en effet de la Russie de 1930 ? Pratiquement rien. Ce n'est que quelques années plus tard avec l'organisation définitive du stalinisme, que les voyages redevinrent possibles. Mais surtout pour les intellectuels déjà conquis à la "cause" et qui ne savait que trop bien ce qu'ils venaient chercher. (7)

[But this particular tale has another advantage: it unites fresh, on the spot reporting and the novelty of this very specific subject. What, in fact, did we know about Russia in 1930? Practically nothing. It is only several years later with the definitive organization of Stalinism that travel to the USSR became possible again. Even this was mainly for intellectuals already won over by the "cause" and who already knew too well what they were coming to find.]

Unsure of where to begin, Maillart turns her observations to the city and the rigors of daily life, habits that will continue to serve her throughout her travels. She notes that although the Soviet government has engaged in multiple building projects, the city's population has more than doubled in less than a decade and a lodging crisis reigns. Maillart can ill afford a month's lodging in a hotel for tourists. Good fortune and especially good preparation lead her to Madame T, Olga Constantinovna Tolstoya, the daughter-in-law of Leo Tolstoy. Madame T had once housed Maillart's friend during a brief stay in Moscow and agreed to rent her niece's room to Maillart during the niece's absence: "Le loyer sera de 50 roubles par mois; lorsque la nièce reviendra, on me cédera, pour la moitié de ce prix, un divan de la salle à manger" (*Parmi la jeunesse russe* 29). [The rent will be 50 roubles a month; when her niece returns, they will give me the sofa in the dining room for half that price.] Taking up residence away from other tourists introduces Maillart to another Moscow, to the realities, both good and bad, of daily life in the Russian capital. Maillart learns to negotiate lines, rationing, and community living. Clearly, she favors the projects of the Soviet government, applauding their initiatives and the class and gender equality that such initiatives impose. She revels at the fact that her questions posed about gender equality seem absurd to Russian workers:

—De quel œil les hommes voient-ils des ouvrières parmi eux? Animosité? Indulgence? Cette question dénote, paraît-il, mon ignorance totale de l'état d'esprit moderne. Les femmes n'essaient pas de concurrencer les hommes. On utilise où il le faut les qualités qui leur sont propres: leur grande précision, leur travail soigné. L'homme n'a pas la sottise de se croire supérieur (pour réclamer une paie plus forte) alors qu'il n'est que différent... (47)[1]

[In what light do the men see the women workers amongst them? Do they show them animosity? Indulgence? This question seemed to indicate my total ignorance about the modern way of thinking. Women do not try to compete with men. Instead, they use their innate qualities, such as their great precision and their neat, careful work, where they are needed. Man is not foolish enough to believe himself superior (so as to ask for better pay) when he is only different.]

Maillart appreciates being on equal footing with her male counterparts. At the same time, Maillart notes that all change comes with a price. Shortages abound in the new Union and everything from bread to boots can be difficult, if not impossible, to obtain:

Crise du cuir. Tout le monde veut des bottes. Sur 160 millions d'habitants, l'URSS compte environ 120 millions de paysans. Autrefois, seuls quelques privilégiés pouvaient s'acheter des bottes; les autres allaient chaussés de sandales d'écorce. Autres temps nouveaux moyens, nouveaux besoins: il faut aujourd'hui botter un continent. (32)

[Leather shortage. Everyone wants boots. Of the USSR's 160 million inhabitants, approximately 120 million are peasants. In the past, only the privileged few could afford to buy themselves boots; the others wore home-made sandals. Another era brings with it new means, new needs: today they have to outfit an entire continent in boots.]

Her Moscow observations introduce Maillart to the complications of the Soviet cause and to the basic tenets of colonization. The rich are no longer the only people wearing boots both literally and metaphorically: Soviet policy obviously dismantled the prevailing class and economic structure. The young people whom Maillart encounter appear to adapt easily to the daily changes proposed by the new regime. Maillart, for her part, seems eager to embrace any change that brings women out of the home and away from domesticity:

> Mais ceux qui tournent le dos à la nouvelle vie et se cramponnent à d'anciennes coutumes pour lesquelles rien n'est organisé continuent à fricoter leurs petits plats, selon leurs petites recettes, entassés chacun dans leur petit coin de cuisine, ponctuant leurs disputes à coups de primus ou de poubelle.
> Au contraire, l'ouvrière accepte sans peine ces nouvelles méthodes qui abolissent le ménage ; elles lui viennent en aide dans sa vie fatigante. (63)

> [But those who turn their backs on the new life and cling to old customs for which nothing is organized continue to cook up the same old dishes, according to the same old recipes, each one crammed into the same old corner of the kitchen, punctuating their disagreements with a bang on the primus stove or the garbage can.
> On the other hand, the woman worker accepts without difficulty the new methods that abolish housework; these new methods help her cope with her tiring life.]

Maillart applauds the changes that liberate women from the drudgery of meal preparation after a full day of work. She goes on to measure the difficulties of the worker's life in Moscow against western standards. Less than a year after having observed countless unemployed German workers, Maillart can more easily accept the rationing imposed in Moscow:

> Puis on me demande si l'ouvrier est heureux dans mon pays, question posée à tout propos. Pour y répondre, mes compétences ne sont pas très grandes ; je dis ceci : l'ouvrier qui travaille est loin d'être malheureux ; il n'est pas rationné dans ses achats, il est libre de changer de patron et de travail, il peut manger de la viande tous les jours. Mais pour les chômeurs innombrables, la vie est tragique. (64)

> [Then they ask me if the worker is happy in my country, a question that is posed constantly. When it comes to an answer, I am hardly an expert. I say the following: the worker who is working is far from unhappy; his purchases aren't rationed, he is free to change employers or jobs, and he can eat meat everyday. But for the innumerable unemployed, life is tragic.]

Maillart recognizes the rewards and hardships of both systems in her effort to remain non-partisan.

Crucial to Maillart's observations of Moscow and the Soviet Union are the circumstances that land her there. As an outsider, Maillart is the celebrated foreigner. Her status opens doors that allow her to further her understanding of the developing republic, and she profits from her position: "Je sais que les circonstances m'aident : en Occident individu banal, ici je suis unique ; par ma seule présence, je revêts une importance démesurée. Je suis la passante qui éveille l'intérêt, qui provoque des réflexions jusqu'alors non formulées" (80). [I know that circumstances are working to my advantage: in the West, I am just another individual, while here I am unique; just my presence accords me inordinate importance. I am the passer-by who piques their interest, who provokes a sort of reflection that had previously been unarticulated.] Maillart displays her admiration and envy for the youth in the communist system. In Maillart's eyes, they have successfully broken the ties to family and duty that weighed so heavy for the author:

> Les jeunes sont libérés de tout ce qui entravait et entrave encore "les autres". Libérés—libres plus justement, puisque eux-mêmes n'ont rompu aucun lien—ils sont indépendants du passé : ils l'ignorent et ne peuvent perdre leur temps à le regretter. Indépendants de la famille et de ses devoirs (ont-ils demandé à naître ?). Indépendants de la religion et des restrictions qu'elle comporte… (80).

> [The young are liberated of all that hindered and still hinders "the others." Liberated—free, actually, because they themselves did not have to break any ties—they are independent of the past: they ignore it and cannot waste their time missing it. Independent of family and its duties (did they ask to be born?). Independent of religion and the restrictions it implies.]

Maillart's age and experience align her with the beliefs of the young Soviets. At the same time, Maillart recognizes that the older generations represent the closest link to life in the capitalist west, and therefore, can best answer some essential questions, especially questions regarding the collective lifestyle that seem laughable to many young people born into the new system:

> S'il juge que vous en valez la peine, un Russe de la génération intermédiaire vous donnera peut-être quelques éclaircissements. Il le peut : se remémorant le passé, il retrouvera les points de vue qui sont nôtres.
> —Mais non, dira-t-il, notre vie collective n'implique pas la fin de l'individualité !" (81)

> [If he thinks that you are worth his time, a Russian of the intermediate generation may help clear things up for you. He can: as he remembers the past, he will rediscover our western points of view.
> —But no, he will say, our collective lifestyle does not imply the end of individuality!]

Impressed with the coexisting values of collectivism and individualism, Maillart gains a new appreciation for the evolving Russian society. In an effort to learn more about conditions in Russia as a whole, Maillart decides to take leave of Moscow.

Eager to embark on a boating expedition after having rowed with a crew team in the capital, Maillart fails in her search for the necessary equipment and a suitable team. She turns to Sovtourist, the organization for proletarian tourism. Not normally open to foreign tourists, Maillart is able to access Sovtourist thanks to her many connections in Moscow:

> Institution merveilleuse : pour des prix dérisoires, on peut aller au Kamtchatka comme à Samarkand. On peut visiter des villes, des fabriques, des fermes, prendre part à une croisière sur la mer Noire en voilier, ou chasser l'ours dans l'Oural. On vous donne à l'avance vos provisions : vous êtes ainsi indépendant des villages qui, pendant ces temps de lutte économique, sont rationnés comme les villes. (85)

> [A marvelous institution: for a pittance, one can go to Kamtchatka or to Samarkand. You can visit cities, factories, farms, take part in a sailing cruise in the North Sea, or hunt for bear in the Urals. They give you your provisions in advance, so that you are even independent of the villages where, during these times of economic hardship, they face rationing like in the cities.]

Impressed with all that Sovtourist has to propose, Maillart pursues their offer. She abandons the water in favor of the mountains, accepting to share in a three-week trip to the Caucasus for the price of 100 rubles. Leaving Moscow will allow Maillart to continue her initiation into the new Soviet ways of life, particularly in areas that have been colonized by the Soviet regime.

Her trip to the Caucasus gives Maillart her first real insights into the enterprise of Soviet colonization. At the same time, it sets the stage for her interpretation of the Other. For this discussion of the Other, it is undoubtedly useful to evoke Gayatri Chakrovorty Spivak's article "Can the Subaltern Speak?".[2] In this most influential piece, Spivak suggests that ultimately the subaltern, configured as the "third-world woman" cannot speak: "Between patriarchy and imperialism, subject constitution and object formation, the figure of the woman disappears, not into a pristine nothingness, but into a violent shuttling which is the displaced figuration of the 'third-world woman' caught between tradition and modernization" (102). This displaced woman has neither place nor voice in the colonial world. As such, someone must speak for her, as Spivak suggests: "The subaltern cannot speak. There is no virtue in global laundry lists with 'woman' as a pious item. Representation has not withered away. The female intellectual as intellectual has a circumscribed task which she must not disown with a flourish" (104). Ella Maillart may not fit the typical description of a female intellectual, but her travels narratives allow her to speak where the subaltern cannot. This task is not a simple one, as Ania Loomba notes in her discussion of Spivak in *Colonialism/ Postcolonialism*: "Spivak effectively warns the postcolonial critic against romanticising and homogenising the subaltern subject" (235). Loomba goes on to contest Spivak's insistence on subaltern silence, noting the difficulty of recovering the subaltern voice as well as the desire to do so (234–5). Loomba concludes this section of her discussion remarking that "we can make visible the importance of subalterns to history without necessarily suggesting that they are agents of their own histories" (244). Ella Maillart turns her gaze to those who remain unseen or unnoticed by Soviet colonial powers, thus making them visible as Ania Loomba suggests. While her initial observations echo those of the colonial power, the evolution of Maillart's understanding of the Other will prove especially noteworthy.

In *Parmi la jeunesse russe*, Maillart, like the Russian travelers who accompany her, initially views the indigenous peoples as ignorant and in need of instruction. In her eyes, those who are not Russian embody the Other, the object of the Soviet colonial efforts. As such, the mountain inhabitants of Upper Suanetia[3] are equated with hoodlums and thieves. Maillart sums up the collective opinion of the Other when she notes: "Quel problème que de soviétiser un Etat paysan totalement illettré" (104). [What a problem to collectivize a peasant state that is totally illiterate.] Tribes from all over the Caucasus comprise this illiterate peasant state. Against their will and without their consent, these many tribes have been absorbed into the greater Soviet Union. Maillart neither protests against nor critiques the Soviet actions. She does, however, bear witness to the initial stages of this transition, giving voice to those not represented by Russian interests. She explains values and traditions very different from the collectivism brought by the Soviets. Maillart carefully notes, for example, the role of honor for the people of Upper Suanetia:

> Un fait est certain : de 1917 à 1924 la vendetta fit 600 victimes parmi les 12 000 habitants de la Haute-Svanéthie. Aujourd'hui, nombreux sont ceux qui s'expatrient pour n'avoir pas à tuer un des leurs.
> Voici les mœurs au milieu desquelles les bolchevistes doivent travailler, et tous leurs efforts tendent à transformer ces conceptions extrêmes de l'honneur. (141)

> [One fact is certain: from 1917 until 1924 the vendetta claimed 600 victims among the 12,000 inhabitants of Upper Suanetia. Today, many live in self-imposed exile for not having want to kill one of their own.
> These are the morals with which the Bolsheviks must work, and all their efforts go to transforming these extreme notions of honor.]

Clearly, Maillart takes the part of the colonizer, sympathizing with the Bolsheviks' difficult task. At the same time, her prose gives voice to people whose story had otherwise remained untold. Maillart's observations contrast traditional lifestyles with the new push toward collectivism. She recognizes that the entire colonial enterprise can be defined in the Soviet efforts to change mentalities: "Admettre de nouvelles idées, moderniser sa vie sont choses possibles; le plus difficile consiste à déraciner les anciennes habitudes logées au cœur des hommes. C'est dans ce domaine que le communisme opère sans cesse" (158). [Tolerating new ideas, modernizing one's life, these are all possible. The most difficult task involves rooting out the old habits instilled in the hearts of men. It is in this domain that communism works endlessly.] Maillart begins to write the Other into the colonial picture. As her travels continue, images of hoodlums and thieves are replaced by pictures of hard working farmers and quiet mountain guides. The evidence of a Soviet presence abound: propaganda sessions are organized and well-attended, peasants are learning to read, their languages transliterated into a Romanized alphabet. Maillart documents the transformation of the unknown Other into a participant in the changing Soviet society. She expresses her continued admiration for Soviet achievements while noting the traditions and lifestyles that may be lost in the name of progress: "Ces coutumes de l'ancien temps subsistent encore aujourd'hui ; parfois juxtaposées aux manifestations de la vie moderne, curieux mélange de deux époques" (151). [Customs from the past still remain today; sometimes they are juxtaposed with expressions of modern life, a curious mixture of two eras.]

Her observations of the Other and their lives will become the subject of her current narrative and future travel books. Maillart's fascination with women and children stems from, at least in part, the fact that she can readily observe them along her journey. Many of the men she encounters would not allow themselves to be in the company of a woman. Because she gives voice to the otherwise silent figure of the colonized, because of her choice of subject, Maillart creates, in a manner of speaking, a feminist discourse for her travels. Her narrative, comprised of photos, observations, and historical notes, offers a rather unique journalistic account of how the people of the Caucasus live and adapt to the changes brought by Soviet colonization.

Maillart concludes her introduction to the Other with the end of her journey. Having crossed the Caucasus, she chooses to spend several days in Sotchi, a resort city on the Black Sea, as the group continues on to Knosta. After weeks of community life and travel, Maillart is eager to be left to her own resourcefulness: "Je serai obliger de me débrouiller, mais j'aime ce corps à corps avec les difficultés : rien de tel pour toucher la réalité, pour savoir au juste comment tout se passe" (176). [I will have to manage on my own, but I like a struggle: there is nothing like it for experiencing reality, to find out how things really work.] After several days of well-earned rest, Maillart returns by train to Moscow, where autumn's cold temperatures have prompted her former housemates to don their coats indoors. The heat has not yet been turned on. Despite the hardships, Maillart's admiration for the Soviet enterprise remains strong. She recognizes that travel in the Soviet Union is undeniably infused with the colonial spirit :

> La société de tourisme a un rôle important : elle oriente les vacances de chaque citoyen selon ses désirs, soit vers le repos, soit vers le voyage. Dans le second cas, elle enseigne comment il faut tirer parti de ce qu'on observe. Il faut préparer le voyage à l'aide des livres que l'on trouve à l'horizon politique, compléter ses connaissances culturelles, se rendre compte de la vie nouvelle qui s'élabore partout . (205)

> [The tourism society plays an important role: it configures all citizens' vacations according to their desires, orienting them either toward rest and relaxation, or toward travel. In the second case, the tourist society teaches people how to take advantage of what they observe. They encourage travelers to prepare themselves with the help of books on politics, to complete their knowledge of other cultures, to recognize the new life that is developing everywhere.]

Maillart, for her part, gratefully took part in the quest to broaden political and social horizons. Her prose, written in praise of the Soviet system, also speaks to and for the many who bore the brunt of Soviet expansionism.

When *Parmi la jeunesse russe* appeared in 1932, its reception reflected the somewhat ambiguous nature of the project. Several critics in Geneva called it red propaganda and referred to Maillart as an avid communist.[4] A review article by Jean Nicollier in the *Tribune de Genève* bore the title "Les mille et un moyens de la propogande sovétique" [The 1001 ways of Soviet propaganda]. Others saw the book as Maillart would have wished, as one that remained, in fact, anti-political. As Eugène Fabre wrote in a 1932 article in *La Suisse* : "Aussi bien son livre est-il, écrit sans préoccupation politique et plus nourri de faits et d'observations que de considérations doctrinaires."[5] [Her book is also written without political preoccupation and is rich in facts and observations rather than dogmatic considerations.] Reviewers in Paris received Maillart's new book with similar enthusiasm, attesting to the growing popular interest in travel writing.

Maillart returns to the Soviet Union two years later with her first book, *Parmi la jeunesse russe*, in hand. The six thousand French francs she earned with the book's publication would finance her current trip.

This time Maillart has no intention of remaining in the city for any length of time. She plans to travel to the eastern reaches of the new Union: "Non. Je veux à tout prix partir pour l'Orient. La vie des nomades me captive. Leur instabilité m'attire, je la sens mienne comme celle des marins : ils vont, d'une escale à l'autre, partout et nulle part chez eux, chaque arrivée ne marquant somme toute qu'un nouvel appareillage(...)" (*Des Monts célestes aux sables rouges* 14). [No. Cost what it may I am determined to go East. The nomad's life enthrals me. Its restlessness pursues me: it is as much part of me as of the sailor. All ports and none are home to him, and all arrivings [sic] only a new setting forth (*Turkestan Solo* 4).] Maillart's ready identification with the nomadic lifestyle pushes her to pursue a formidable journey: from Moscow to Kazalinsk (Kazakhstan) and onto the Tien Shan before descending to the ancient cities of Bokhara and Samarakand. Her political naïveté and sheer willpower allow her to conclude that such a voyage is even possible:

> Peut-être ma personne insignifiante, doublée d'un passeport helvétique, pourrait-elle circuler librement dans le pays? J'arriverais alors à savoir si les soulèvements sont soutenus par les Anglais ou les Russes, par un fanatisme musulman ou par un réveil nationaliste ; et celui-ci chercherait-il à recréer l'ancienne unité turco-mongole? (*Des Monts célestes aux sables rouges* 15)

> [Was there a chance, I wondered, of my insignificant person, backed by its Swiss passport, being able to travel freely through the land? Then I should know whether it was Britain or Russia, or Mussulman [sic] fanaticism, or possibly a nationalist awakening, whose object was to restore again the ancient Turki-Mongol unity, that was behind the revolts. (*Turkestan Solo* 4)]

Armed with her Swiss passport, Maillart sets out in search of answers to her questions about the Soviet colonization of the east: who stands behind the uprisings? How successful have Soviet projects of collectivism been in the far reaches of the empire? Has colonial rule destroyed the nomadic life that Maillart so desperately seeks? Such are the questions that guide both her writings and her travels.

Maillart's search for nomads, for the Other, will also initiate her search for self. In fact, she hopes to find the simplicity that eludes her in European society in 1930: "Il faut tout réapprendre afin de pouvoir apprécier. C'est la notion que nous avons plus ou moins perdue : le prix de la vie. Près des peuples simples, montagnards, marins ou nomades, les lois élémentaires s'imposent à nouveau. La vie retrouve son équilibre" (*Des Monts célestes aux sables rouges* 33). [Everything must be relearnt again, before life can be truly gauged. What life is worth is a conception we have lost, more or less. But in contact with primitive, simple peoples, mountain dwellers, nomads, and sailors, it is impossible to ignore the elemental laws. Life finds its equilibrium again (*Turkestan Solo* 22).] At this point in her career, Maillart looks to the simplicity of a more authentic lifestyle, one not burdened with modern society's demands, and to the freedom of movement associated with nomadic tribes.[6] Her feminist identification with the nomadic lifestyle predates the postmodern nomadic itinerary described by Rosi Braidotti by fifty years.[7] Later in her life, Maillart will look inward for this elusive peace. For now, however, the anticipation of the voyage may be worth the journey itself, as Maillart suggests: "Je vais vers des contrées désolées, sans arbres et sans maisons. Après des mois passés dans une solitude millénaire, je pourrai juger ce que vaut la multitude. Dormant sous le poids du ciel, je saurai ce qu'est un toit. Cuisinant sur un feu de crottin, je connaîtrai la valeur du bois" (*Des Monts célestes aux sables rouges* 33). [My way leads towards desolate lands, treeless and empty of habitations. I shall pass months in a solitude as old as the hills, but then I shall be able to judge what crowds mean to me. With all the weight of the heavens over my sleeping body, I shall learn what a roof is, and cooking over a fire of dung I shall learn the true worth of wood (*Turkestan Solo* 22).] Maillart's *Des Monts célestes aux sables rouges* records the lifestyles of tribes very foreign if not unknown to her western readers and begins the author's personal search for meaning and understanding. This arduous trek thus leads to the first steps of the lifelong inner journey.

The first steps out of Moscow prove to be, at least practically speaking, the most difficult. Maillart must scramble to find an expedition that she may join in an effort to reach the mountain ranges of Kazakhstan and the Kirghiz Republic. The very passport that she hoped would serve her well thwarts her initial efforts: the few scientific expeditions heading east do not want to be burdened with a foreigner. Supplies and train tickets are nearly impossible to procure in a city besieged by rationing. Nonetheless, Maillart manages to get wind of a small group leaving for the Tien Shan. Because the group hesitates to assume responsibility for the young Swiss in the remote mountain regions, Maillart must find an acceptable alternative that will allow her to join them at least at the outset. Maillart places a calculated call to the leader of the group: "comme vous le savez, j'ai mon billet pour ce soir; aussi je décide de partir quand même. Mais je voulais vous demander si je pouvais me joindre à vous jusqu'au haras dont vous parliez sur l'Issik-Koul. Là, j'étudierai la vie collectivisée pendant que vous irez dans les montagnes. Conciliabule, les autres sont d'accord" (26–7). [You remember I told you that I already have my ticket for to-night. Well I've decided to go in any case. But I should like to ask whether I may accompany you as far as the stud-farm you mentioned near Issik-Köl. Then, while you were away in the mountains, I could stay and study how collectivization is working. A deliberation follows. The others agree (*Turkestan Solo* 15).]While Maillart has no intention of remaining behind, her conciliatory tone opens the door for her to accompany the small group, two couples planning to explore the multiple summits of the Tien Shan. Her recently published book, which she offers to two of her companions who know French, takes care of the rest. Once they have read *Parmi la jeunesse russe*, the members of the team are eager to have Maillart join them. As Maillart notes:

> Aujourd'hui mon livre m'a rendu un fameux service—plus important que de caler ma pharmacie dans mon sac. Je l'ai emporté, pensant que, dans une ville ou l'autre, il pourrait me servir d'introduction, puisque j'en suis dépourvue. Mila et Volodia, qui savent le français, l'ont lu et en ont sans doute parlé à Auguste. Le chef me dit avec un sourire qui me transporte d'aise : —Nous allons voir comment tout s'arrangera ; peut-être pourrez-vous quand même venir avec nous. (*Des Monts célestes aux sables rouges* 36)

> [Today my book did me signal service…much more use in fact than stuffing my medicine box in my sack… I had taken a copy with me, thinking that in some town or other it might prove a credential, since I had no others. Mila and Voldya, who knew French, had read it, and doubtless Auguste had been told about it, for with a smile that quite transfixed me with delight he said: 'We are going to see whether something can't be done: perhaps it will be possible for you to join us after all.' (*Turkestan Solo* 25)]

So begins Maillart's journey to the mythical Tien Shan. Ultimately, she hopes to visit the fabled Sinkiang in China, off-limits to foreigners and suffering the repercussions of an ongoing civil war.

The initial stages of her journey help inform Maillart of the political realities of the period. She secretly stops to visit dissidents in order to learn more about life under Stalin's regime: "Puis je veux à tout prix rendre visite à un déporté trotzkyste dont j'ai appris l'adresse par cœur. Mais je ne veux pas que mes camarades le sachent ; cela pourrait leur déplaire, ils ne savent pas que je suis sans opinion politique, et poussée seulement par la curiosité. Ils craindraient aussi qu'on pût les accuser d'avoir prise avec eux une personne louche(…)" (42). [After which I determine at all costs to visit a Trotskyist exile whose I address I have taken care to memorize. My intention must be kept secret from my companions, however, for they might not like it. They do not know I have no political convictions whatever, and that curiosity is merely my motive. Also they might be afraid of possible accusations of having taken a politically unsound person with them(…)(*Turkestan Solo* 30).] In order to ensure her safety and the safety of her companions, Maillart's visit to Vassili Ivanovitch must be accomplished secretly. Maillart leaves the group for a solitary walk in Frounzé in search of her Russian acquaintance. What she discovers gives her a first lesson in Stalinist politics. As Ivanovitch explains to his Swiss friend:

—Je suis gratte-papier dans un bureau, de quoi gagner ce que je mange. Mais si je fournis un travail plus intéressant, même en heures supplémentaires, vite on me change de service. Il me faut faire timbrer régulièrement mes papiers à la police ; autrement, on est assez libre. Patients ? Oui, nous le sommes sans effort ; mais impossible de savoir où sont les nôtres, s'ils sont déportés, s'ils peuvent s'organiser(…) Où va notre pays ? Pour peu que Staline continue ainsi, tout est perdu. (44)

["I scribble away in an office here, and so I earn my keep. But if I do work of a more complicated nature, even after hours, I am immediately posted to another job. My papers have to be regularly endorsed at the police office. Apart from that I am free enough. Patient? Oh yes, we are, and it isn't difficult for us; but it's impossible to find out where the others are, whether they have been exiled or not, or whether they are able to organize(…)Where is the country going? If Stalin doesn't slow down soon, it's all up with us." (*Turkestan Solo* 32)]

Ivanovitch thus sheds light on the nature of Stalin's campaign, of which few details were known in 1932. Ivanovich goes on to explain to Maillart the situation of the indigenous peoples:

Ici bien sûr, les nationaux (nom donné aux indigènes) détestent les Russes, qui sont les colonisateurs. On leur a bien dit que les Russes d'après la Révolution étaient tout différents, mais eux-mêmes n'ont pas encore beaucoup à dire dans le gouvernement...Oui, je sais, ils ont leurs journaux, leur langue, leurs écoles, mais tout doit rester immuablement dans la ligne dictée de Moscou. (44-5)

[In this place, of course, the Nationals (which is the name the natives go by) detest the Russians who are colonizing them. They've had it impressed on them that the post-revolution Russians are altogether different, but they themselves so far have had little say in the government...Yes, I know they have their newspapers, their language, schools; but they can never, never depart from the line laid down by Moscow. (*Turkestan Solo* 32)]

This dose of political reality helps Maillart see more clearly the dual nature of the Soviet enterprise. In fact, Maillart's subsequent observations indicate that Soviet colonial efforts brought few advantages to the indigenous population of Central Asia. Collectivism sought to put an end to the nomads' wanderings and replaced regional crops and livestock with the cultivation of cotton. Maillart points out later that Soviet colonialism effectively continues Tsarist policies that began years earlier. The only difference came down to who enforced the governmental changes:

Pour les dénomadiser on les a installés parfois dans des colonies organisées par des Russes après 1916, mais ils ne savent pas bien en cultiver les jardins. Ou, au contraire, ils faisaient partie d'un sovkhose où ils estimaient ne pas avoir obtenu tout ce qu'on leur avait promis : ils sont partis, reprenant leur vie de nomades. (78)

[Since 1916 many attempts have been made to wean them from their nomadic lives and settle them in colonies founded by Russians. But they show little interest in cultivating the earth. On the other hand, they do at times enrol themselves in some collective farm, but as a rule they soon leave to resume their old nomadic lives, complaining that they have not received all the benefits they were promised. (*Turkestan Solo* 63–4)]

The disappointment in the proposed changes by the Soviets encouraged the nomads of the region to return to their traditional lifestyles whenever possible. However, new political frontiers and land divisions decided in Moscow made this return difficult. Between 1916 and 1930, the native Kirghise, for example, became political pawns, floating between Russian, Chinese, and later Soviet rule. As Maillart explains: "Après le soulèvement national de 1916, alors que les Cosaques exterminaient les Kirghises, tous ceux qui le purent passèrent au Sin-Kiang. Mais là-bas, les Chinois n'avaient aucune

raison de protéger ces Kirghises musulmans, d'origine turco-
mongole : leur bétail fut volé peu à peu. Dénués de tout, ils décidèrent
alors de rentrer chez eux. C'était l'hiver, ils périrent en route par
milliers." (132) [After the national uprising of 1916, when the
Cossacks were exterminating the Kirghiz, all who were able fled into
Sin Kiang. But the Chinese inhabitants saw no reason for offering
protection to these Kirghiz-Mussalmans of Turki-Mongol origin, and
by degrees their herds were stolen from them. Stripped of everything,
they decided to return whence they had come. It was winter and they
perished in thousands on the way (*Turkestan Solo* 113).] When Maillart
asks some of the nomads she encounters about the Soviet influence,
the response she receives is hardly surprising:

> Alors je pose la questions que j'ai sur la langue depuis longtemps :
> —Soviets, iakchi (bons) ?
> —Iamâne...Oh, iamâne. At, koï, djok ! Francia, koï bar ? (Mauvais, oh
> mauvais. Chevaux, moutons, point. France il y a des moutons ?) Pour eux,
> bien sûr, les efforts et le but que les Soviets poursuivent sont
> incompréhensibles ; il faut attendre que leurs enfants puissent expliquer ce
> qui se passe. (97)

> [I take the opportunity to ask a question that has long been on my tongue:
> "Soviet, iakchi?" (Good).
> "Iamane...Oh, iamane. At, koï, djok ! Francia, koï bar ?" (Bad, oh bad.
> Horses, sheep, none at all! France, are there sheep? Obviously, to them, the
> efforts and objects of the Soviet Government must be quite
> incomprehensible. All that can be done is to wait until their children can
> explain to them what is happening. (*Turkestan Solo* 82)]

Maillart recognizes that the Kirghiz see failure in the Soviet initiatives,
yet she stubbornly continues to support the intent and the execution
of the Soviet mission to collectivize, failing to recognize the true irony
of the situation. The collective but self-contained groups of nomads
traveling with their yurts functioned with marvelous precision,
involving all members in their communal living project. Yet, they
could not negotiate modern-day borders and the Soviet call to fall into
line as part of the larger whole. Unwilling to conform, the Kirghiz
were thus condemned to years of fighting and unrest, as Maillart
observes: "Révoltés à nouveau, les Kirghises affamés se vengèrent
comme ils purent. C'était la fin de la grande année 17 ; peu à peu, les
Russes démobilisés revinrent du front, devenus Rouges après la
révolution. Trouvant à chaque pas des marques de ravages, ils

usèrent de représailles, se livrant à leur tour à des exécutions" (132). [Once more the now starving Kirghiz rose up in revolt and avenged their wrongs as best they could. It was the end of the great year 1917. Little by little the demobilized Russians filtered back from the Front, all Reds now after the Revolution. On every hand signs of destruction met their eyes. They too began to make reprisals, and in their turn started shooting their captives (*Turkestan Solo* 113).] Maillart thus sheds light on both sides of the colonial dilemma and the Kirghiz people. She accumulates first-hand observations and historical information to relate the stories of the colonizer and the colonized. Again, by giving voice to the colonized Kirghiz and other indigenous people, Maillart allows for an alternative to the dominating power of Soviet politics in the early 1930s.

As Maillart works to record these two competing discourses, the voice of colonial power and that of the nomadic people who figure as the object of that power, she also configures the Other. The Other first comes to the reader in the form of places, later as faces and people. Maillart constructs the people and places she encounters through a combination of observation, story telling, history, and legend. She tells of the Issik-Koul, the enormous lake that lies before the expanses of the Tien Shan:

> Quoique l'Issik-Koul ait une superficie vingt fois supérieure à celle du lac Leman, aujourd'hui, au coucher du soleil, j'ai trouvé une analogie entre les extrémités occidentales de ces deux lacs. Les paysages aussi sont éclairés sous le même angle. Ribatchi, au bout du lac, à une quarantaine de kilomètres d'ici, serait une Genève innocente, à peine née ; le majestueux Tierskeï évoque la chaîne de Savoie qui délègue aussi, près de l'eau, une grosse bosse au dos plat comme celle du Salève. Le Kunguei, sur les dernières pentes duquel nous sommes couchés, rappelle le Jura et sa ligne continue. (58)

> [Although Issik-Köl is twenty times larger than Lake Leman, with the setting sun I seem to find a likeness in the western extremities of both lakes and the country about them. Ribatchi, some twenty-five miles away at the end of the lake, would be an unspoilt Geneva barely born. The majestic Tereskei evoke the Savoy ranges, and like them end up at the water's edge with a large flat-topped mound which reminds me of Salève. Finally, the Kungei, on whose slopes we now compose ourselves to sleep, recall the Juras and their unbroken line. (*Turkestan Solo* 45)]

The lake, compared to the Lake Geneva of another era, thus evokes a familiar picture for her Swiss and French readers. To add to that image, Maillart tells the stories of past kings of the region, legends that recall the classical myths of western tradition. Her observation of the Kirghiz and Uzbek men and women round out her description:

Il y a de nobles Kirghises—à tout seigneur tout honneur—à maigre barbe pointue, yeux acérés, portant le bonnet de velours bordé d'astrakan gris ou noir, large couronne régulière...Leurs femmes portent un énorme turban d'une blancheur éclatante: l'étoffe aux spirales très fines et parallèles...Ce sont les "manaps", les patriarches, chefs de tribu de qui dépendaient souvent des centaines de yourtes. (66)

[There were the Kirghiz of noble birth—all honour where it is due—with straggly pointed beards, piercing eyes, and velvet bonnets on their heads which, with their grey or black astrakhan brims, seemed like large round crowns...These are the "Manaps," or patriarchs, chiefs of their tribes, on whom often hundreds of yurts depend. Their wives wear enormous turbans, dazzling white, the material wound in close and narrow spirals. (*Turkestan Solo* 53)]

Maillart thus introduces her discussion of the indigenous people she meets. What begin as more general observations move toward the specific as Maillart spends more time among the nomadic tribes. As the expedition moves from the city into the shadows of the Tien Shan, Maillart is better able to study the communities of yurts that unfold before them. She recognizes that their very lifestyle is put into danger by the Soviet push toward collectivism.

Maillart and her fellow travelers are invited to remain with the families living in the yurts as they advance toward the mountain summits. Here the young woman Patma impresses Maillart with her quiet intelligence: " Nous dialoguons par gestes. Elle s'appelle Patma, m'offre du koumouiss puis du lait caillé. Elle est intelligente : elle ne répète pas en vain cinq fois de suite et de plus en plus fort des questions incompréhensibles, comme le font ses compatriotes." (90). [Our conversation is carried on by gestures. Her name is Patma, and she offers me koumiss and then sour milk. She is intelligent: she does not ask the same incomprehensible question five times running and always on a louder note, like the rest of her compatriots (*Turkestan Solo* 75).]Maillart elaborates upon their return to the yurts several days later:

La digne Patma est chez elle. J'aime son visage las dont j'ai vu les traits doux tantôt éclairés d'en haut par un blanc rayon de soleil tombé du toit, tantôt d'en bas par les lueurs rouges du feu. Son mari, cordial, sympathique avec ses trois poils noirs de barbe au menton, me demande naturellement où est mon mari. Chaque fois qu'il me parle, il me tape sur l'épaule, s'imaginant qu'ainsi sa question descendra plus vite dans mon entendement. (96)

[I pay a visit to the worthy Patma. I have grown fond of her resigned face whose gentle features I have watched, now illumined from above by the white rays of the sun through the hole in the roof, now from below by the flickering fire. Her cordial, likeable husband, a few odd hairs to his chin, naturally asks me where my husband is. Whenever he addresses me he taps me on the shoulder, convinced, no doubt, that in that way it will penetrate my understanding quicker. (*Turkestan Solo* 81)]

This close look at women and family life becomes a defining feature of Maillart's travel books. She identifies with these people at a certain level, treasuring their common desire to move freely and travel uninhibited.

Maillart remains, however, part of the expedition, dependent on her comrades coming and goings. She is also nagged by money problems, having spent more than expected on her last minute preparations:

J'ai encore un souci qui ne me lâche pas : le manque d'argent (mon voyage a duré six mois, de juillet 1932 à janvier 1933, et je disposai en tout et pour tout d'une somme légèrement inférieure à 6000 francs français de l'époque…). Auguste avait dit à Moscou qu'il fallait avoir mille roubles pour ce voyage. Je les avais alors et je crus que tout était en règle, sans réfléchir qu'au cours de ma dernière folle journée je dépenserais trois cents roubles pour faire mon équipement, acheter vivres et billet. (75)

[A last anxiety continues to gnaw at me: shall I have money enough?[8] Auguste had told me in Moscow that I should need a thousand roubles for the trip. And as I had about that sum at the time, everything seemed all right. But I had not taken into account the fact that my last hectic day in Moscow would cost me three hundred roubles to complete my equipment, purchase food, and buy a railway ticket. (*Turkestan Solo* 61)]

In danger of not having enough money to continue, Maillart sends a telegram to a friend in Moscow requesting 500 rubles. In the meantime, her fellow travelers will lend her any necessary money.

Maillart is thus able to advance through the summits of the Tien

Shan on horseback. Her skiing prowess allows her to climb one of the peaks and ski down in a mere seven hours, half the time that it took her companions who set out only on foot. She inspires admiration and even envy among her colleagues. As Maillart proudly notes, Capa cannot contain her astonishment: "—C'est n'est pas possible en si peu de temps, dit Capa. Mila rit en me regardant et cligne de l'œil dans la direction de Capa : on lit en elle à livre ouvert, elle est désappointée de ne plus être la seule à avoir été au Sari-Tor" (109). ["It isn't possible in so short a time," says Capa. Mila laughs as she looks at me, and winks in Capa's direction. You can read her like an open book. She is disappointed not to have been the only woman to have scaled Sari Tor (*Turkestan Solo* 93).] Maillart and her companions continue on to the mountains that separate the USSR from the Sinkiang region and China. Maillart can see the forbidden land before her, and there she hesitates:

> Voici à mes pieds l'un des buts que je m'étais proposés : les montagnes chinoises habitées par les Kirghises, le Sin-Kiang bouleversé par les courants opposées…J'ai avec moi tout ce qui m'est essentiel, à l'exception de mon sac de couchage. Je pourrais partir seule pour Tourfan, quelques kilomètres à pied ne sont pour m'effrayer. Seulement, je n'ai pas de visa. (133)

> [Here at my feet is one of the objectives I had set myself in coming so far: the Chinese mountains inhabited by Kirghiz, and Sin Kiang in the turmoil of opposing currents…I had everything with me I really needed, all but my sleeping bag. There was nothing to stop me setting off alone for Turfan: and the few miles on foot were in no wise frightening. The only thing was my lack of visa. (*Turkestan Solo* 114–5)]

Recalling stories of immediate imprisonment for those without papers, Maillart decides to finish this leg of her journey in the company of her newfound friends. They succeed in selling the horses with enough of a profit to recuperate the money Maillart owed. After a final failed effort to procure the visa necessary to enter Sinkiang, Maillart decides on an alternate route. Sinkiang will have to wait for her next journey: " J'essaie en vain de savoir où est M. Ba Tou Tchin, consul du Sin-Kiang. Le sort est jeté : j'abandonne définitivement l'idée d'aller en Chine. Je partirai pour Tachkent et les villes légendaires du Turkestan : Samarcande, Boukhara et Khiva" (156) . [In vain I try to discover Mr. Ba Tou Tchin, the consul for Sin Kiang. The die is cast. I give up definitely the idea of going into China. I shall leave for Tashkent and the legendary cities of Turkistan: Samarkand, Bokhara, and Khiva (*Turkestan Solo* 136).]

The second part of *Des Monts célestes aux sables rouges* is consecrated to Maillart's solo travel through Turkistan,[9] its ancient cities, and the red desert. Alone, Maillart pursues her study of the progress of Soviet colonialism. Her observations remain mixed: she cannot help but praise the Soviet efforts to modernize, in particular concerning their work with women. At the same time, she voices her criticism of the destruction of tradition and the unquestioned implementation of Soviet method. Maillart's consciousness begins to shift, and her criticism of the Soviet enterprise becomes noticeably more pointed.

Alone in Alma-Alta, on the frontier of The Kirghiz Republic and Kazakhstan, Maillart visits another political exile. He has lived in Alma-Alta for a year now, sent there after being accused of participating in a religious sect. In Alma Alta, he works at the university as a professor of history. He finds his students are strong, not unlike the students he taught in Russia:

> —Que pensez vous de vos élèves indigènes ?
> —Ils sont tout aussi intelligents que les Russes, même parfois plus persévérants...
> —Croyez-vous qu'ils seront bientôt assez formés pour se gouverner seuls ?
> —Certainement, rien ne les en empêchera et je pense que d'ici quelques années, ils se passeront même des Russes.
> —Et vous pensez qu'alors ils marcheront dans les mêmes voies politiques que les dirigeants soviétiques ?
> —Certainement. (160)

> ['What do you think of your native students?'
> "They are quite as intelligent as the Russians, and certainly at times more industrious..."
> "Do you think it will be long before they are mature enough to govern themselves?"
> "Certainly not, there is nothing to prevent them becoming so, and it seems to me that within the next few years they should even be able to dispense with all Russians."
> "And do you think that then they will see eye to eye politically with their Soviet administrators?"
> "Certainly." (*Turkestan Solo* 140)]

The deportee's high opinion of his students coincides with Maillart's own ideas. Like her, the professor believes that the Soviet path will be the path chosen by the colonized. Neither Maillart nor the professor doubt the validity of the Soviet mission here. Soon after, however, Maillart will begin to question the Soviet colonial presence.

Maillart's change of opinion develops out of her continued interest in the indigenous groups of the region. She compares the nobility of the Kazak people to the character of their Russian compatriots: "Combien les Kazaks, que j'ai pu qualifier de primitifs, écrasent tous ces Russes par leur dignité innée, témoignage certain d'une culture qui laisse encore des traces" (169). [How superior these Kazaks, with their native dignity, which bears certain testimony to a culture whose traces still persist, seem to all these Russians. And to think I once thought them a primitive people (*Turkestan Solo* 148).] Clearly, Maillart admires the nomadic Kazaks, but does she look at them as the romantics might have viewed the noble savage? Is she guilty of romanticizing the nomad? I would argue that no, Maillart's view is better informed, her experience with the nomadic people she encounters genuine rather than invented. Her solo travels allow her to meander at her own pace, and Maillart takes her time winding through the streets of Tashkent where she observes women hidden by heavy veiling:

Tout me surprend : les étroites rues pavées, coudées en labyrinthes, le nombre de femmes voilées, silhouettes de cercueils dressés, avec le contour raide et monolithique du parandja. Sur les têtes, un paquet ou une corbeille en équilibre. Cela n'a aucun sens de parler de voile : c'est treillis qu'il faudrait dire, tant est rigide et sombre cette toile en crin de cheval qui leur blesse le bout du nez, qu'elles pincent entre leurs lèvres lorsqu'elles se penchent pour regarder la qualité du riz qu'on leur offre, le regard ouvrant seulement filtrer lorsque le tchédra est perpendiculaire devant les yeux. (171)

[It all astonishes me: the narrow, stone-paved streets, labyrinthine, the numbers of veiled women, in the stiff, unbroken lines of their 'paranjas,' looking like silhouetted upright coffins, with some package or basket balanced on every head. It is nonsense to call them veils: trellis-work is far more to the point, so dark and rigid is the horsehair which scarifies the tips of their noses, and which they pinch in their lips when they bend down to see what quality of rice is being offered them, for their sight is only able to filter though when the 'chedra' is hanging straight down in front of them. (*Turkestan Solo* 150)]

Maillart travels in part to seek out her own independent voice and clearly her encounters with women hidden from society leave her ill at ease. Here in particular, Maillart supports the position of the Soviets who wish to free women from their traditional garb. Maillart's opinion falls in line with the voice of many late twentieth-century feminists when confronted with similar issues in places like Afghanistan and North Africa. Like her philosophical descendents, Maillart finds herself caught between western values and those of the traditional society.

Forever the curious journalist and traveler, Maillart pursues this subject when she interviews Faïsoulla Khodjaief, president of the Uzbek Council of Commissioners at the time:

> —Dites-moi, dans le vieux Tachkent, presque toutes les femmes sont encore voilées ? Avec vos grandes réformes féminines, croyez-vous que la femme soit plus heureuse ? On dit que la prostitution s'est développée depuis l'émancipation.
> —L'abandon du tchédra ne compte pas dans cette libération et ne peut être qu'un symbole. On y a attaché trop d'importance, ce qui a créé des drames de familles. L'important, c'est la maturité intérieure, développée par les écoles, la propagande, le travail rétribué rendant la femme indépendante du mari. (198)

> ["Another thing! In old Tashkent practically all of the women still go veiled. Do you think women are happier as a result of the great reforms that have been introduced on their behalf? I'm told that prostitution has increased since their emancipation."
> "The fact that the 'chedra' has been cast aside has no particular significance: it must be taken as a symbol of liberation merely. All the emphasis has been laid on the fact—hence the family complications. What is of real significance is psychological maturity, and that we are achieving through our schools, our propaganda, and wage earning, which makes the woman independent of her husband." (*Turkestan Solo* 175-6)]

His answers hardly satisfy Maillart, who has heard before that the veil is merely a symbol. Maillart realizes that she cannot break through his official demeanor and she finds this failure especially frustrating: "L'interview est terminée, sans que j'aie réussi à établir un contact direct entre nous, quoique nous ayons souvent parlé sans l'aide d'un interprète. Dans l'antichambre une vingtaine de patients attendent leur tour d'audience et me regardent avec férocité : je suis restée une heure et demie dans la grande salle" (199). [The interview was over, and not once had the man revealed himself or abandoned his official tones; not once had I succeeded in establishing any real contact between us, though we had often spoken without the help of an interpreter. In the ante-room some twenty people patiently wait their turn for an audience, and look ferociously at me as I pass. I had been in the audience chamber an hour and a half (*Turkestan Solo* 177).] Her journalistic inquisitiveness does not stop with her somewhat unsatisfactory meeting with the Uzbek president. As she travels to the ancient cities of Samarakand and Bokhara, Maillart continues her research on women and their changing roles. In particular, Maillart wants to enter into direct contact with working women rather than discuss their welfare with their Soviet supervisors. Her discussion with the female director of a local sewing and weaving cooperative provides Maillart with yet another official version of the women's stories :

> Oui. Il faut faire attention. La libération de la femme crée du mécontentement dans les ménages. Les vieilles qui gagnent s'en moquent. Pour les jeunes, c'est toujours le même rengaine : " Je ne veux pas que tu sortes comme ça ", dit l'homme. Nous instituons une petite cour pour juger les scènes de famille...Seule l'instruction finira par ouvrir les yeux aux hommes. (226)

> ["Yes: we must go carefully. The liberation of women has created discontent in the home. The old women who gain by it jeer at it, and as for the young, it's always the same story: 'I won't have you go out like that,' says the man. We've established a small court for dealing with these family differences. It's the husbands who have to be made to see reason...But education will open their eyes in time." (*Turkestan Solo* 200–1)]

Maillart, however, has heard enough of the party politic and seeks to enter in direct contact with the women of the region. As she complains to her Russian friend, Maroussia: " —Je veux entrer en contact plus direct avec les femmes indigènes, en ville et à la campagne. J'aimerais trouver un village où je puisse habiter et travailler aux champs avec les femmes" (227). ["I want to enter into more direct contact with the native women, both in town and country. I should like to find a village where I could live and work in the fields with the women" (*Turkestan Solo* 201–2).] Maillart's wish will go unrealized. When a friend leads her to the home of an Uzbek man where Maillart can meet with the women at her leisure, her visit is cut short. Maillart learns that the master of the house is ill with typhoid only after she has shared his bowl of tea. Unwilling to risk her health further, Maillart leaves quickly, never answering her own questions about the changing conditions of women.

If Maillart remains torn between Soviet modernization and Islamic traditions with regard to women, she shows less ambivalence toward Soviet reforms in agriculture. She recognizes that the so-called reforms have made daily life nearly impossible in the provinces. The people she meets in Tachkent only confirm her observations :

> Ah ! vous venez de là-bas ! Chez vous, en Frankistan, le riz pousse-t-il ? Savez-vous ce qu'ils ont fait ici ? Ils ont donné l'ordre de planter le coton partout. Alors, la charrue a passé, détruisant nos petites rigoles de rizières, établies et entretenues depuis longtemps avec tellement de soin. Après, quand ils ont vu que le blé ne venait pas facilement, ils ont dit : "Replantez un tiers de riz ." (175-6)

> ["Ah you come from far away. In your country, in Frankistan, do you grow rice? Do you know what they've done here? The order was given to plant cotton all over. So the plough went everywhere, blotting out the tiny irrigation channels of the rice fields that were made so long ago and kept up with such care. And after that, when they saw the wheat did not grow easily, they said to us, 'Replant a third with rice.'" (*Turkestan Solo* 154) Translation modified.]

The flawed Soviet operation leaves the indigenous people starving. Their rice fields have been destroyed in favor of cotton or wheat. When wheat crops fail, they are told to replant rice. The absurdity of the situation is readily apparent, and Maillart poses a pointed question to President Faïsoulla Khodjaief during her interview with him:

> —Encore une chose m'intéresse : croyez-vous qu'un Khirghise nomade puisse se transformer en prolétaire ?
> —Bien sûr, parce qu'il voit tous les avantages qu'il y gagne : il ne gèle plus en hiver, il reçoit du pain, du sucre, des bottes, une paie fixe, une vie organisée, des distractions. Ce sont les mêmes avantages qui ont décidé nos paysans à remplir les conditions du Plan pour la culture du coton. (198)

> ["Another thing interests me particularly. Do you think it possible for a nomad Kirghiz to turn himself into a town-dwelling proletariat working eight hours a day?"

"Certainly, when he realizes all the advantages it means to him. He no longer freezes in winter; he gets bread, sugar, boots, a stable wage, a regular existence, amusements. These advantages were the main factor in deciding our peasants to carry out the 'Plan' for cotton cultivation." (*Turkestan Solo* 176)]

Both Maillart and her esteemed interviewee must recognize the imminent failure of the Soviet plan. Khodjaief chooses to ignore the signs, but Maillart becomes decidedly more critical of the Soviet agricultural reforms. As she notes at the end of the interview: "J'aimerais objecter ce que Faïsoulla sait aussi bien que moi, certainement : les habitants du Turkestan se plaignent de ce que, dans la période d'adaptation actuelle, la vie est impossible" (198). [I should have liked to make an objection, which Faisulla must certainly have been as clearly aware of as myself: namely, that the inhabitants of Turkestan were bitterly complaining that, while the process of adaptation was going on, living conditions had become practically impossible. (*Turkestan Solo* 176)] People are hungry, and cotton will hardly provide food for the masses.

Even the Soviet party line begins to wear on Maillart. She is loathe to attend another party gathering with a friend in Tashkent. Every gathering sports the same party propaganda:

Je n'ose pas lui dire que ces éternelles conférences m'ennuient, elles sont toutes identiques, que ce soit à Naltchik, à Karakol ou à Moscou, elles me font penser aux moulins à prières tibétains : nécessité de développer la culture chez les indigènes, d'éduquer les masses, d'édifier le socialisme grâce au nivellement des classes, le socialisme dont seul l'avènement sauvera le monde de la faillite capitaliste.

Même si c'est notre salut à tous, il faudrait l'orchestrer avec un peu plus de variété. (177)

[I dare not tell him that these eternal lectures bore me. They are all exactly the same, whether at Nalchik, Kara Kol, or Moscow. They make me think of Tibetan praying wheels: "importance of developing culture among the natives of educating the masses, of constructing Socialism by levelling the classes, Socialism whose triumph alone will save the world from capitalist bankruptcy!"

Even if all our salvations depended on it, surely it could be orchestrated with a little more variety. (*Turkestan Solo* 155–6)]

With that ongoing refrain in mind, Maillart positions herself in a sort of colonial conundrum. Unable to support the wide range of Soviet reforms, Maillart is nonetheless unwilling to abandon the progress that she associates with the Soviet campaign. Ultimately, Maillart cannot give up some of her fundamental notions of justice and progress. She remarks that the past and the present are constantly at odds in the eastern-most reaches of the USSR: "A chaque pas, le XIVe siècle se dresse en face du XXe ; le droit du plus fort a toujours primé et il faut créer de toutes pièces la notion de justice. A chaque pas, la force de l'habitude s'oppose à la force de volonté apportée par les Soviets" (245). [At every step the fourteenth century rises to face the twentieth. Here, right has always been to the mightiest, and the notion of justice for all must be inculcated from the very bottom. At every step the force of habit opposes the will to do that the Soviets have brought with them (*Turkestan Solo* 218).] Likewise, Maillart works hard to reconcile past and present in her own mind. Her admiration for Soviet colonial efforts is clouded by their unyielding push for progress that continues to ignore the needs of the indigenous peoples. Maillart shows, however, the true nature of the colonial dilemma: the overwhelming majority of colonial powers believed with great fervor in the merits of their civilizing mission. Maillart's travel book dismantles some of the racist perceptions that drove the colonial movement. Her descriptions and observations attest to noble, intelligent, and industrious peoples, not simpletons in need of western wisdom. At the same time, Maillart cannot help but believe in the changes brought about for women and the disenfranchised.

The other driving force behind Maillart's narrative voice is her simple love for travel. She seems to revel in the complications of moving from place to place in this society that functions under rationing and non-western notions of efficiency. She is welcomed in Turtkul, for example, as the first foreign tourist in the newly-founded tourist office: "Dans un autre bureau, sur la même place immense, le président de la Société de Tourisme prolétarien, un jeune Karakalpak à moustaches, est transporté de joie à ma vue : —Vous êtes notre première touriste. Camarades ! Une touriste : une touriste de Paris, de France ! —Qu'est-ce que c'est que touriste? lui demande son secrétaire" (284). [In another office, situated in the same immense square, the president of the Society for Proletarian Tourists, a young Karaakalpak with moustaches, goes into transports of joy at the sight of me. "You are our first tourist. Comrades! A tourist, a tourist from Paris, from France!" "What's a tourist?" asks his secretary (*Turkestan*

Solo 255).] The constant newness, the invariable presence of the unknown, stimulate Maillart and her reader. As she notes toward the end of her journey: "Partir, c'est revivre. Tout recommence, je ne sais pas ce que je vais traverser. Le soleil se lève, rouge comme il s'est couché hier. L'air étincelle de givre en suspension et j'avance dans une réalité plus belle qu'une féerie" (317). [To set off! That is like being born again. Everything begins anew: I do not know what lies in front of me. The sun rises red, as it set last night. The air sparkles with frost, and I advance into a reality more lovely than a fairy tale (*Turkestan Solo* 284).] Her final departure during this trip will be on the back of a camel as she joins a caravan to cross the desert known as the Red Sands. This final crossing signals the end of her journey, the return to western cities and the regular monotony of daily life. As Maillart so aptly states: " Il n'y a plus d'imprévu possible, le vrai voyage est terminé" (336). [There is no likelihood of anything unexpected happening now: the real journey is over (*Turkestan Solo* 301).]

The publication of *Des Monts célestes aux sables rouges* by Grasset in Paris in 1934 met with a warm reception and immediate success. A best seller in France, Maillart's travel book brought her near celebrity status. Maillart herself became a standard feature in the women's magazines and an example for the growing feminist press. As Germaine Grey notes in the May 1934 *Minerva*: "Le gros livre illustré d'Ella Maillart est un document rare qui doit prendre une place de choix dans le coin de l'Aventure. Mais il est surtout un témoignage étonnant de ce que peuvent l'énergie, la volonté féminine mises au service d'un claire intelligence et d'une curiosité jamais comblée."[10] [The thick, illustrated book by Ella Maillart is a rare document that should take its well-deserved place among adventure books. But more than anything else, this book bears witness to what energy and feminine will-power can do when combined with a clear intelligence and a never-ending curiosity.] In Switzerland, Maillart found enthusiastic followers. Eugène Fabre, reviewer for the daily *La Suisse*, called Maillart's latest book "un passionnant récit de voyage, aventureux à souhait."[11] [a passionate travel narrative, with all the adventure one could wish for.] The English version, *Turkestan Solo*, translated by John Rodker and published by Putnam's in 1935, met with success on both sides of the Atlantic. The *New York Times* review dating from February 1935 sings Maillart's praises, albeit somewhat tongue in cheek:

> Through her narrative she interweaves a thread of history that keeps the reader aware of what was happening in these mountains and deserts in the days of Attila, or Jenghis Khan, or later years. The entire book is written with very great detail, often picturesque and colorful, but so truthful that it does not spare the reader the filth, the vermin, the discomforts, the crudities of the daily life, none of which, however, did Miss Maillart seem to mind in the least, so keen was her constant enjoyment. ("A Woman in Turkestan")[12]

The indomitable spirit that carries Maillart throughout *Des Monts Célestes aux sables rouges* becomes a trademark for her prose and travel. Whereas *Parmi la jeunesse russe* represents an initial query into the world of travel writing, *Des Monts Célestes aux sables rouges* serves to establish Maillart's career as a travel writer. Indeed, with success will come more travels. Even as these reviews appear in Paris, Geneva, London, and New York, Maillart has already begun her next trip to Asia, preparing to cross China in a final effort to reach the Sinkiang region.

Maillart's *Des Monts Célestes aux sables rouges* and *Parmi la jeunesse russe* stake a claim for the Swiss adventurer in the world of twentieth-century travel narratives. Her foray into colonial discourse gives voice to those who bear the brunt of the colonial movement. In the process, Maillart creates two engaging tales that attests to the historical realities of the 1930s in the ex-Soviet Union. She bears witness to the beginning of colonial expansion and the end of certain indigenous lifestyles. Ultimately, her first two books accomplish several of the authors goals: she may not reach Sinkiang, but her travel narratives offer a timely look at a world virtually unknown to her western readers. The arm chair travelers who read Maillart's books thus share in the search for the Other, the quest for justice, and perhaps most of all, the pleasure of the journey.

Notes

1   Maillart does not elaborate on the assumed and innate gender differences that this quotation implies.

2   See Gayatri Chakrovorty Spivak's "Can the Subaltern Speak?" (1985) in *Colonial Discourse and Post-Colonial Theory: A Reader*. For further, related analysis of Spivak's discussion, see Ania Loomba's book *Colonialism/ Postcolonialism*.

3   Region of the Caucuses on the west coast of the Black Sea, located between the cities of Batoum, near the Turkish border, and Naltchik. Suanetia is the geographical term used by John Rodker in 1935 in *Turkestan Solo*, the translation of Maillart's *Des Monts Célestes aux sables rouges*.

4   The archives at the University of Geneva house a collection of newspaper and magazine articles that describe the reception of *Parmi la jeunesse russe* at the time of its publication. Most of these articles are clippings from the original newspaper or review, and do not always include date and page information. This is reflected in the bibliographical entries noted at the end of my study.

5   Special thanks to Madame Françoise Pittard at the archives of the Bibliothèque populaire et universitaire in Geneva (BPU) for her help and advice regarding the book reviews in the Ella Maillart collection.

6   I will discuss Maillart's identification with nomadic peoples and some of the competing theories on nomads and the postcolonial world at length in chapter five of this study.

7   See Rosi Braidotti, *Nomadic Subjects: Embodiment and Sexual Difference in Contemporary Feminist Theory*.

8   The English translation includes the following footnote, included directly in the French text: "I must apologize for attaching so much importance to this matter. But my journey lasted some six months, from July 1932 to January 1933, and all the money I had available was francs to an amount equivalent to rather less than £75" (*Turkestan Solo* 61).

9   Hence the title of the English translation, *Turkestan Solo*. The spelling of the region today in English is generally written as Turkistan.

10   Germane Grey's article is catalogued with the "coupures de presse" in the Ella Maillart collection cited above and does not include the page numbers of the clipping.

11   Eugène Fabre's review of *Des Monts Célestes aux sables rouges* dates from May 22, 1934; the clipping does not include page numbers.

12   The NY Times review, entitled "A Woman in Turkestan," is also housed with the "coupures de presse" in the Ella Maillart collection of the BPU in Geneva ; the clipping includes neither the author of the review nor the page number.

Chapter Four

Diverging Perspectives:
Ella Maillart and Peter Fleming
on China

For seven months in 1935, Ella Maillart and Peter Fleming traveled across the vast expanses of China, first via train and truck, later via horseback, by camel, and on foot. Fleming, the striking, self-assured reporter from London and older brother of the famous Ian Fleming, joined forces with Maillart on this memorable trek. Maillart's *Oasis interdites* (1937) and Fleming's *News from Tartary* (1936) present two versions of this singular journey that follows their fateful meeting in Peking. [1] These travel narratives provide details of a voyage noteworthy not only for its itinerary—Maillart and Fleming venture into the region of Sinkiang (Tartary) in northwest China, off-limits and closed to foreigners at the time, before reaching India—but also for their diverse perspectives and understanding. In fact, the travelers' gaze reveals as much about the colonial world as it does about China in 1935. This chapter will focus on the differences in the points of view presented by the two narrations and the reasons for this divergence.

These travelogues offer a very specific look at the construction of the identity of self and the Other. The authors embark on a literary and metaphorical voyage in an effort to "discover" both China, its people, and perhaps themselves. The progression of the construction of these identities depends on the movement and rhythm associated with their journey. Their perspectives are gendered, culturally informed, and constantly subject to the changing reality of the voyage. As Sidonie Smith explains in the first chapter of *Moving Lives: Twentieth-Century Women's Travel Writing*:

> Narrating travel by foot, plane, locomotive, or automobile, the travel
> narrator negotiates the dynamics of and contradictions in the drift of
> identity, and reveals the ways in which modes of mobility—engines of
> temporality, spatiality, progression, and destination—are (un)defining.
> But she may also define the meaning of a particular mode of motion in
> new and different ways, and in doing so, disentangle travel from its
> masculine logic. (28)

A more detailed analysis of these texts should, in effect, allow us to identify and "disentangle the travel from its masculine logic," as Sidonie Smith suggests. In fact, Maillart's approach to travel in general distinguishes itself readily from that of Fleming, suggesting a gendered, feminist mode of discourse and movement. The construction of travel and the self progresses as the narrator comes into contact with the Other. Through the revealing looks at people and places encountered, Maillart and Fleming's construction of the Other assumes a variety of forms, including the familiar Other or the companion, as well as the exotic, foreign Other. Do their narrations ultimately reflect or redirect the colonial view of the Other? Is the woman traveler's vision feminine or feminist? This analysis will work to identify the narrative strategies used by Maillart and Fleming in order to construct the image of self and the Other in the context of the travel narrative.

Before considering *Oasis interdites* and *News from Tartary*, let us return to a more general discussion of the travel narrative as a genre. The travel narrative, as noted earlier, remains a genre that is difficult to categorize. Blurring the lines between an autobiographical account and an ethnographic study, travel narratives borrow from journalism, the novel, and history. How then, can we distinguish between an anthropological study and a travel narrative? Patrick Holland and Graham Huggan explain this distinction in their book *Tourists with Typewriters: Critical Reflections on Contemporary Travel Writing*:

> Travel writing is self-consciously autobiographical, intentionally
> anecdotal, and (in some cases) deliberately ethnocentric, whereas
> ethnography has tended until recently to play down the personality of
> its author, to substitute scientific for anecdotal information, and to
> critique ethnocentric assumptions behind the study and description of
> "foreign cultures" while remaining aware at the same time of its own
> prejudices and biases. But distinctions between travel writing and
> ethnography remain, at best, problematic. (11)

For Peter Fleming but especially for Ella Maillart, the travel narrative vacillates between autobiography and ethnography. Maillart criticizes the ethnocentric approach whereas Fleming represents all that is ethnocentric and English. At the same time, the two juxtapose political commentary and humorous anecdotes, history and personal observation. For Holland and Huggan, the travel narrative thus becomes a "pseudoethnographic" text (12); indeed, these two travelogues may be read as "pseudoethnographic" studies for the armchair traveler reading from the comfort of home. Both Ella Maillart and Peter Fleming write for a particular audience, one that cannot yet travel with ease to the far-off ports of Asia. As a result, their travel narratives should provide the reader with up-to-date political commentary as well as an entertaining if not escapist narrative.

This particular genre lends itself well to the styles of Fleming and Maillart. For Fleming, well-known traveler and journalist, the travel narrative allows him to move easily between the personal and the public. His account, characterized by a consistently ironic tone, emphasizes his dry English humor. While Fleming shows no inclination to criticize his own ethnocentric approach, he does consider it his duty to inform the reader of certain socio-political realities. Maillart, however, lacks the professional experience that Fleming brings to writing. As noted earlier, by the age of thirty, Maillart had already worked at a variety of professions, including navigator, sailor, tutor, actress, skier, traveler and writer-journalist. In 1935, at the time that these two travelers decide to cross China from west to east, Maillart is still looking to define herself, to find her place in the world: she writes in order to continue her travels, rather than traveling in order to write. As such, the travel narrative, the loose mix of autobiography and ethnography, allows her to pursue her search for self and indulge her desire to be an ethnographer.[2] For Ella Maillart, the travel narrative becomes at once an autobiographical and yet objective form of writing. As Holland and Huggan explain, the genre is particularly well-suited to such a situation:

> Travel writing...is a distinctive autobiographical form; like other autobiographies, it seeks to make retrospective sense out of discrete experiences: to convert a mishmash of impressions into a coherent narrative. But unlike most autobiographies...travel narratives are less concerned with recuperating, or reinventing, a single self than with following the trajectory of a series of selves in transit. (14)

Maillart follows this trajectory in writing of her travels, in writing of herself. The development of the self in transit, as Holland and Huggan suggest, should allow for the continued development of Fleming and Maillart's world views. Their understanding of China, its people, and their travels will depend, however, on their individual relationships with the colonial world and their inevitably gendered perspectives.

In the last fifteen years, a number of authors have explored the role of gender and the woman traveler in the colonial and post colonial world.[3] Sarah Mills recognizes that the conditions of production determine the difference between the narrations of men and women travelers (40), and that women were literally left out of the equation, with neither the authority, nor the space to write in or on the colonial world. Women travel writers thus belong to a group of eccentric women in the margins, and Maillart is, in many ways, no exception. She never marries, and chooses an independent and somewhat precarious lifestyle. Both the conditions of literary production and the conditions of literary reception—where women travel writers carry less authority than their male counterparts—separate her from Fleming before and after their trek across China. In fact, only the voyage and their common itinerary link the two writers and the two texts.

As we consider the work of Fleming and Maillart, the gendered agent of the narration inevitably becomes part of the discourse. As Holland and Huggan explain: "The traveling subject is always gendered, always embodied, and always active: recognizing this, many women travel writers. . .have turned their narratives into critical explorations of both the potential for and limitations of female agency in the contemporary world" (132). Even if Ella Maillart wrote neither to draw attention to the condition of women in Asia in general, nor to fight against hegemonic stereotypes of the colonial world, her gaze inscribes humanist, feminist observations throughout her text thus presenting a vision of the world very distinct from that of her colleague, Fleming.

The voyage through the heart of China reminds us of expeditions and explorations prior to the contemporary era, when the difficulty of getting around characterized all modes of transportation. Their journey thus recalls the glorious past rather than the tourist-oriented side of travel. Whereas Fleming travels in order to rejoin India and the British Empire, Maillart leaves behind the modern world in search of the life of the nomad, a way of life that she interprets as authentic and true. Like Alexandre David-Néel in Tibet or Isabella Eberhardt in Algeria, Ella Maillart travels far from the city, far from all that is familiar. Sidonie Smith writes about David-Néel and Eberhardt and their choice of "pre-modern" spaces in *Moving Lives*: "The Maghreb, the mountains of Tibet…these are vast 'premodern' spaces, uninhabited by urbanized peoples. They are spaces far distant from overcrowded metropolitan centers, spaces as yet unmarked by the rampant and rampaging signs of progress, by the tracks of locomotives, the pavement of superhighways" (31). Like David-Néel and Eberhardt, Maillart sets off on foot, horseback or by camel, hence close to the ground: "Travel by foot or by animal attaches the traveler bodily to the ground. An intimate of the ground, she imagines herself an intimate of the people of the land" (Smith 31). David-Néel and Eberhardt literally assume the costume of the local people, thus accepting identities other than those conventionally accorded to women in the West (Smith 32). Maillart never disguises herself, but nonetheless, during her travels she leaves behind the preconceptions of the Occident in order to begin to understand and to know better China and the Other. As Smith explains specifically when speaking of the identity of the woman traveler: "In becoming another kind of subject, in grounding herself in another's identity, the traveler imagines herself un-becoming Western. Shedding conventional identities and behaviors, stripping away the residue of modernity, she becomes other to her ordinary, unheroic 'feminized' self" (32). Even though Maillart may never have adhered to the conventional and pre-determined role of women early in the twentieth century, her travels nevertheless permit her to leave behind her western identity. During the voyage, she forms another idea of self, of Other.

The construction of this Other relates specifically to the traveler's perception of the Orient as well as to the concept of exoticism. The exoticism of the nineteenth century and Pierre Loti influences but no longer defines the attitudes of travelers in the 1930s. As Charles Forsdick explains in his article "Sa(l)vaging Exoticism: New Approaches to 1930s Travel Literature in French:"

> Since it was coined just over 150 years ago, the term 'exotisme' has been subject to steady semantic shifts between two poles: one signifying an

> exotic-ness essential to radical otherness, the other describing the process whereby such radical otherness is either experienced by the traveller from outside or translated, transported, and finally represented for consumption at home. (30)

The travel writer of the 1930s thus goes beyond the identification "radical otherness" in its exotic context and undertakes the job of interpretation, responsible for communicating this interpretation of the Other to readers at home. For Fleming, this transformation remains fairly simple: a professional journalist, he presents foreign places and peoples from the English perspective, a perspective that has not yet been contested or brought into question by the Second World War. Indeed, both Fleming and Maillart write during the 1930s, a period sometimes considered the heyday of travel and travel writing.[4] This period coincides with the final years of the English empire and the reign of the colonial powers. As Forsdick notes:

> This decade [1930s] represents, therefore, a key period before the rapid changes brought about by the war and by the effects of its aftermath — the principal amongst these being the sudden reconfiguration of relations between Europe and its others particularly in the light of the severing of direct colonial links and the forging of new patterns of cultural interrelations that either undermined or refuted Western hegemony. (32)

Fleming, representing the *Times* of London and all that is English, never questions his national identity as one that renders him superior to others. As Karen Veit observes in her comparison of several travel writers, including Fleming and Maillart, Fleming looks to establish a certain image of himself for the reader:

> [In *News from Tartary*] narrative persona, travel plot, and description of the setting develop as a result of the author's aim of fixing in the reader's mind an image of himself as an experienced traveller, a successful journalist, a patriotic British subject, and a likeable fellow in the prime of his masculinity — in short, heroism and importance personified." (111)

Ella Maillart, on the other hand, maintains a more ambiguous rapport with the cultural interrelations noted by Forsdick. As a Swiss woman traveler and writer, she does not carry with her the same prejudices as her English colleague. Her understanding of exoticism and the exotic links the individual and place, the individual and Other. She does not vacillate between romantic and barbaric constructions and conceptions of those she encounters, but rather works to make the exotic more familiar to herself and to her readers. She brings into question the colonial conquest in her approach as well as in her attitude to her travels. For Maillart, the voyage itself takes the place of colonial occupation and appropriation. Consider the theory proposed by Forsdick when he speaks of the travel narrative of the 1930s:

> The term 'exotic' is recovered as a linguistic shifter, no longer describing a restricted series of fixed locales and a bank of oft jaded images; the notion of exoticism becomes dependent on reflexivity and reciprocity and develops into a potential tool for considerations of intercultural contact and of one of the principal modes of such contact: travel itself. With this understanding of exoticism there is a further shift from the notion's pejorative overtones of cliché and control to a potentially more complex understanding of the interaction between individual and place. ("Sa(l)vaging Exoticism" 42)

Maillart and Fleming's travel narratives allow the authors to interpret the rapport that develops between themselves and China for their European readership. Exoticism thus no longer simply serves as an indicator of colonial power, but helps author and reader to analyze and explore this rich and complex cultural interaction. The radically different, if not antithetical approaches that Maillart and Fleming use to evaluate and reflect upon exoticism will lead to two very diverse interpretations of a single voyage.

Exoticism and its interpretation add to the autobiographic and ethnographic research that the travel narrative already entails. According to Jean-Marc Mourra in his article "Mémoire culturelle et voyage touristique:"

> Le récit de voyage correspond à une littérature de la révélation, rapatriant l'inconnu dans le quotidien du voyageur...Il possède l'inaliénable privilège d'un regard contemplant un monde inouï qu'il s'approprie avant de le révéler aux lecteurs afin d'asseoir sa différence. (271)

> [The travel narrative corresponds to a literature of revelation, repatriating the unknown into the daily routine of the traveler...He possesses the inalienable privilege of a gaze that contemplates a world so unheard of that he takes possession of it before revealing it to the reader, so as to establish his authority and difference.]

Peter Fleming presents a vision of China that highlights his desire for control, consistent with the male, colonial tradition, while Elle Maillart writes to question and revaluate this same tradition.

If, as Jean-Didier Urbain suggests, "travelling is about changing life stories before it is about changing places" (156), Maillart and Fleming's trek first traces the lines of an autobiographical study and figures secondly as a political or ethnographic commentary. This is undoubtedly true for the two narrations that present these authors/narrators and their traveling companions as they make their way across China. We will see Fleming's impatience and his burning desire to arrive at their final destination in India, an attitude that contrasts starkly with the slower pace of Maillart, who savors every moment of the journey. The circumstances that lead to this voyage are such that Fleming and Maillart must accept their lot and each other.

This compromise hardly suits Maillart or Fleming at the outset. An odd pair, both insisted that traveling alone would be more to their liking, and indeed, they travel together rather unwillingly at the beginning, making the best of unforeseen circumstances upon their arrival in Peking. Maillart, for her part, had just returned from Russia and the farthest reaches of the newly founded Soviet Union, after having camped and caravaned among the nomads of Turkestan and the Kirghiz Republic. Her book, *Des Monts célestes aux sables rouges* or *Turkestan Solo*, had earned her some fame among her cohort of travelers, writers, and journalists in Paris and Geneva. Taking advantage of her newly established reputation, Maillart managed to convince the French magazine, *Le Petit Parisien*, to send her to China as a special correspondent. As the English title of her book suggests, solo travel suited her, and she never planned to join her expedition with Fleming, the young and dashing writer for the *Times* of London. For his part, Fleming proved equally wary of joining up with a female companion. His dreams of traveling across China to the Himalayas never included a fellow traveler. His last book, entitled *One's Company*, made it all too apparent that Fleming was content to move forward alone. Yet when the two acquaintances met in Peking, it became obvious that their paths would cross and keep them together:

> De Pékin il [Fleming] avait projeté de revenir en Europe par la Mongolie et Ouromtchi, inspiré en partie par l'admirable livre d'Owen Lattimore, le dernier étranger qui, en 1927, ait réussi à passer de la Chine aux Indes. Mais arrivant à Pékin après avoir visité Shanghaï et Tokio, il

venait de se rendre compte que son itinéraire était irréalisable. M'entendant parler du Tsaidam et des Smigounoff, il me dit froidement: "En effet, c'est par là que je rentre en Europe. Si vous voulez, vous pouvez venir avec moi(...)"
—Pardon, répondis-je, c'est mon itinéraire à moi, et c'est moi qui vous emmènerai si j'y trouve avantage.
La controverse dure encore ! (*Oasis interdites* 18).

[He [Fleming] had planned to return from Peking to Europe by Mongolia and Urumchi. The idea was partly suggested by Owen Lattimore's admirable book, *The Desert Road to Turkestan*, Lattimore having been the last foreigner (it was in 1927) to succeed in getting across China to India. Arrived in Peking, after visitng Shanghai and Tokio, Fleming had just begun to realize that his proposed itinerary was impracticable. Hearing me speak of the Tsaidam and the Smigunovs, he had said coldly: "As a matter of fact, I'm going back to Europe by that route. You can come with me if you like (...)"
"I beg your pardon," I had answered. "It's my route and it's I who'll take you, if I can think of some way in which you might be useful to me."
The controversy still rages. (*Forbidden Journey* 8)]

Despite their stated preferences for solo travel, Maillart and Fleming leave together in the hopes of attaining the forbidden region of Sinkiang.

Even before they had crossed the first one hundred kilometers, it becomes clear that the two travelers envision China and their trek across the vast nation very differently. Fleming moves forward in order to reach India and the British Empire once again. His attitude and his behavior during their journey indicate that Fleming's interests lie not in his desire to know a foreign place and its people, but in his wish to learn more about the political situation in Sinkiang, linked to India via commerce and trade. Likewise, Sinkiang's position to the north of neighbor Tibet, an English protectorate at the time, provided yet another point of interest for Fleming. As Michel Delon explains in his short article dedicated to *Oasis interdites* on the occasion of its republication as part of Payot's *Voyageurs* series in 1989: "Peter Fleming, en bon sujet de Sa Majesté, veut savoir ce qui se passe à quelques semaines de chameau des Indes britanniques" (59). [Peter Fleming, loyal subject of Her Majesty, wants to know what is happening in British India, just a few weeks away by camel.] His voyage as well as his very identity are defined in relation to the colonial mission and his English nationality.

Maillart, on the other hand, does not participate in the same way in the colonial endeavour, as explained in previous chapters. According to Delon, "humainement curieuse de ces tribus perdues qui ne connaissent pas la mer" (59) [humanly curious about these lost tribes that do not know the sea], she prefers the slow pace of the caravan and its camels in the steppes and mountains of Asia to cosmopolitan Europe. As Maillart explains in *Oasis interdites*:

> En somme, nous n'envisageons pas les choses sous le même angle. Peter, tous les soirs, me répète comme un refrain: 'Soixante lis de moins d'ici Londres!' C'est pour me taquiner, et je le prie de se taire, car je veux oublier que le retour est inévitable. Je suis même sans désir de retour. Je souhaiterais que le voyage pût se prolonger toute la vie. (77)

> [Yet we did not see things from the same angle. Every night Peter would repeat his refrain: "Sixty lis[5] nearer to London." He did it to annoy me, and I would tell him to shut up, for I wanted to forget that we had, inevitably, to return home. I even lost the desire to return home. I should have liked the journey to continue for the rest of my life. (*Forbidden Journey* 88)]

While Maillart's meandering is an end in itself, Fleming's travels function as a means to an end. These very different perspectives thus embody diverse approaches to a single journey.

The remaining pages of this chapter will focus specifically on a comparative analysis of *News from Tartary* and *Oasis interdites* in an effort to understand better these two divergent points of view. According to Delon "un voyageur qui écrit nous en apprend plus des pays qu'il traverse qu'un écrivain qui voyage. Mais deux voyageurs qui écrivent parallèlement, dans une concurrence amicale, donnent aux paysages qu'ils évoquent une rare profondeur stéréoscopique" (59). [A traveler who writes teaches us more about the countries that he is crossing than a writer who travels. But two travelers writing simultaneously, in a friendly rivalry, give a rare, stereoscopic depth to the landscapes they see.] This discussion will look to identify specifically the strategies and the presuppositions of Fleming and Maillart that lead to a stereoscopic vision of China in 1935.

News from Tartary, on the one hand, builds a narrative based on the number of kilometers crossed and the quantity of wild game shot: "We did a longer stage that day, though it was only six hours and not a full one. . .There were a few hares about, and I missed one badly with the .22″ (112). Everything is quantified in Fleming's narration: even the long but inevitable periods of waiting are punctuated by seemingly endless games of solitaire, as he notes:

> The principal business of the day was to collect rumours about our fate; but we knew from experience that it was a mistake to address ourselves too early to this task, thereby exhausting the day's small stock of hope and leaving us with many hours to kill. So for a time I played endless games of patience on the k'ang while Kini[6] read or sewed or wrote up her diary. (78)

Fleming prides himself in assuming the masculine perspective. Likewise, as Fleming presents measurable, verifiable facts, he thus assures the objectivity of his narration.

In addition, Fleming provides a series of well-informed comments on the complex political situation of the region, again guaranteeing the authenticity of his narration. Furthermore, the tone taken by the narrator leaves no doubt that Fleming is an expert in an area where the reader can only assume amateur status. Consider the following quotation from the sixth part of *News from Tartary*, entitled "The Desert Road:"

> Politics are tiresome things at the best of times; and for the ordinary reader the politics of Asia are particularly tedious and distasteful. Their relevance to his own destinies is non-existent or at best remote…Moreover, the politics of Asia are richly encrusted with polysyllables scarcely pronounceable and so similar in their outlandish unfamiliarity that the ordinary reader has the greatest difficulty in distinguishing between a place, a political leader, and a prevailing wind. (245)

Fleming thus distinguishes clearly between himself, the well-traveled expert in colonial affairs, and the average reader, who need not venture beyond the living room thanks to the author's detailed description. In Fleming's defense, few readers knew anything about the far-off region of Sinkiang, and hence would rely on the author's description to learn about the politics of the area. Fleming, in turn, accepts to explain the situation in a simple, yet comprehensive manner, recognizing this as the fundamental goal of his travels: "In so far as our journey had a serious object, it was to find out what was happening in Sinkiang" (245). Fleming explains in the course of the thirty pages that follow the diverse foreign interests in the area—

Chinese, Russian, and English—as well as their influence and ability to wield power over the Tungan and Turki people of the region (271). This detailed and complex assessment of the political scene contributes to the authenticity of Fleming's text: the traveler who has succeeded in entering and then leaving the territory that is off-limits to foreigners undoubtedly becomes the best source of new, accurate information. This ostensibly neutral political commentary thus assures the objectivity of Fleming's narration.

Ella Maillart, in *Oasis interdites*, also shares information on the political situation of the region with the reader. Like Fleming, Maillart presents her commentary along with an historical context for the current situation and the fundamentally diverse attitudes of the various parties implicated in the affairs of Sinkiang:

> On ne peut s'empêcher de songer à l'attitude toute différente des Tibétains, qui au Sud, s'isolent dans leur bouddhisme mystique, et ne laissent le XXᵉ siècle pénétrer chez eux que goutte à goutte pour l'assimiler progressivement. Au Nord, au contraire, la Sibérie, fouaillée par le deuxième Plan quinquennal, nourrit le machinisme. Prise entre deux tendances opposées, que va faire l'Asie Centrale encore musulmane ? (49)

> [One could not help wondering about the Tibetans away to the south, whose attitude is quite different. They shut themselves up in their mystical Buddhism and only allow the twentieth century to penetrate drop by drop, so as to be assimilated gradually. On the other hand, Siberia in the north, under the lash of the second Five Years Plan, is being mechanized. What, exposed between two influences, and still Moslem, is Central Asia going to do? (*Forbidden Journey* 49)]

This brief analysis considers the various attitudes toward modernization and colonization thus lending the same impression of objectivity to Maillart's narration. Her commentary, however, does not lead to a more informed understanding of English expansionism and political interest. Instead, Maillart questions the future of central Asia, where modernization, ancient cultures, and religion will all come into conflict. Like Fleming, Maillart uses her expertise to shed light on a situation unknown to the average reader. Unlike her traveling companion, Maillart focuses on the role of the indigenous people, not on the colonial power.

The real difference between *Oasis interdites* from *News from Tartary*, however, lies in the human component of the text. Maillart, who writes her narrative based on people and places encountered, adds to these observations historical details and descriptions of the path they have followed. Maillart does not work to quantify her text, but rather to humanize it. In order to know and understand better nomad life, she wants to devote herself entirely to the journey: "Mais je m'étais si complètement intégrée dans la vie de la piste, à la vie des bêtes, à celle des éléments, qu'il me semblait l'avoir toujours menée. C'était l'Occident qui me paraissait irréel" (80). [But there, I was so completely absorbed in the life of the trail, the life of the beasts, of the elements, that it was as though I had always been living it. It was the west that seemed unreal (*Forbidden Journey* 93).] This desire to immerse herself entirely in her travels may seem naïve, but the sincerity of her remarks ring true throughout her travelogue. Maillart even notes that her happiness comes from the encounters with nomads and the lives of the indigenous peoples:

> Devant notre tente, plantée au bord d'un ruisseau limpide, des femmes vêtues de longues et droites robes de lin, viennent nous offrir des plats de bois pleins de lait caillé, et, dans une nappe, de jaunes galettes de maïs tout imprégnées encore de la chaleur du four. Si jamais j'ai vécu un instant de bonheur sans mélange, c'est là, devant ces dons parfumés et savoureux de la nature, entourée de visages bienveillants. (139)

> [We pitched our tent on the bank of a limpid stream. Women, wearing long, straight linen garments, came with wooden bowls of sour milk and, in a cloth, yellow bannocks of meal bread hot from the oven. If ever I have had a moment's unmixed happiness it was there, surrounded by kindly faces and with those sweet-smelling, savoury, natural gifts before me. (*Forbidden Journey* 170)]

Maillart's happiness does not extend to her traveling companion, who hardly seems to notice the indigenous peoples in his haste to arrive at his goal. Clearly, he mingles with the same people observed in Maillart's text, but his colonial gaze does not see in the same way. Maillart reproaches both herself and Fleming for their failure to slow their pace and observe all they can. She regrets not spending more time among the nomads of the distant regions through which they travel. Moreover, she does not hide her disdain for "cette manière de voyager où l'on va de l'avant sans avoir jamais le temps de faire la connaissance de rien. Mais Peter veut arriver le plus vite possible" (190). [And I made no bones about telling Peter what I thought of people who travel too fast and took no time to learn anything about anything. But Peter was crazy to get on as quickly as possible (*Forbidden Journey* 240).] Fleming does not deny the pleasures of life in the caravan—he savors their ill-tempered mornings, their tea and barley breakfasts (123)— but nonetheless focuses on the future rather than the present of the voyage. Even his card games serve to predict their chances of arriving at their goal: "I only know one kind of patience and I don't really like playing that, but by now I had perfected a method of foretelling the expedition's future by the results I got. If it came out (which hardly ever happens with me) we were going to get to India" (154). He and Maillart thus present fundamentally contradictory positions vis-à-vis the voyage and the people they meet, and these positions constitute an essential difference in the construction of the two texts.

The analysis of the Other distinguishes *News from Tartary* from *Oasis interdites* as well. Fleming's ethnocentric approach is certainly striking: he never really leaves England behind him as he crosses Asia on horseback and camel. His observations are colored by his western perceptions of civilization and intelligence, and he never questions this perspective, as is evident when he speaks of the Mongolian people:

> The Teijinar Mongols were surly, bearish people. They looked wilder and woollier than their neighbours of Dzun, and none of them spoke a word of Chinese…Dust and wind and sun had given them a crusted look; their small bloodshot eyes glittered redly in their broad dark faces. A Mongol on foot lacks his native centaur dignity, and these people, shambling half furtive and half truculent through the thickets, suggested, more strongly than any human beings I have ever seen, the poor monster Caliban. (150–1)

Fleming has a difficult time classifying the Mongolians encountered as people rather than monsters. He finds fault with them for failing to speak Chinese, again typical of his colonial mentality. Fleming's unflagging belief in his own cultural superiority never leaves him, and he measures all of his interactions with an English yardstick, so to speak:

> Sometimes a few of us would ride on and sit down in the shelter of a hollow to smoke; the long-stemmed, small-bowled pipes would be passed from hand to hand, and mine with them if it was asked for, for I saw no reason to be haughty and exclusive in this matter. When people know no customs but their own, and when their own customs are few

> because of the extreme simplicity of their life, it is only courteous to
> respect those customs when you can. Besides, my pipe was a great
> marvel to them. (125)

Fleming reads Mongol customs as innately inferior to his own English
experience. As a result, Fleming, while perhaps fascinated by the
exotic nature of the indigenous people with whom they interact,
hardly considers them worthy of lengthy description in his
travelogue.

Fleming pays more attention to his traveling companion
throughout the course of his narrative. The author assures the reader
that his companion, while both courageous and useful, nonetheless
took care of the "feminine" aspects of their voyage. He goes so far as
to propose a list that explains the division of labor (169), in order to
confirm for the reader that he was responsible for neither cooking nor
cleaning. According to Karen Veit, "One has the feeling that while the
narrator hastens to show his great respect for Ella Maillart on this trip,
he is in fact demonstrating how glad he is that she 'behaves so well'
and does not cause any trouble" (114). Fleming recognizes that
without Maillart, he might not have traveled far. Nonetheless, he
relegates the so-called feminine tasks to Maillart while he focuses on
more dignified, masculine activities, like hunting. When discussing
supplies and preparations for the journey, Fleming notes:

> Our supplies and equipment, though they would have made any
> respectable modern expedition sick with laughter, proved completely
> adequate to our needs and to conditions on the road. For this the credit
> goes to Kini, who ran the commissariat with unfailing foresight and
> whose housekeeping instincts, though perhaps rudimentary by the
> highest feminine standards, were an excellent foil to my contemptuous
> improvidence in these matters. (109)

According to Fleming, Maillart thus assumes responsibility for all
that is deemed feminine in their preparations and travels. Fleming, for
his part, asserts his own incompetence in this sphere. On the road like
in England, Fleming divides his world into masculine and feminine,
into familiar and foreign. It is hardly surprising that Fleming
completed his baggage with tobacco and a bottle of Worcestershire
sauce: his English point of view keeps him, at least metaphorically,
close to home. This may explain why Fleming devotes as many pages
to the discussion of arms and rifle calibres as to nomadic peoples. By

reinventing his English pastimes to suit his trans-Asian trek, Fleming can assure his colonial superiority and remain focused on his ultimate goal: arrival in India and thus a return to the outskirts of the British Empire.

Whereas Fleming seeks to recreate the habits and comforts of home in their trek across China, Maillart looks to those around her in an effort to observe the nomadic people's routine, much as she had in Turkistan and the Kirghiz Republic. She relishes the so-called primitive life and the hardships it may bring:

> Je retrouve une partie de mon passé et je continue en quelque sorte le voyage commencé au Turkestan russe…je n'ignore pas la recherche des bêtes égarées à la poursuite de la pâture, ni le silence des nuits où les yeux brûlent d'avoir trop regardé dans le vent. J'aime cette vie primitive où je retrouve la faim qui transforme en joie solide chaque morceau mis sous la dent. (*Oasis interdites* 76–7)

> [I, on the other hand, was going back to a chapter in my own history. In a sense I was only prolonging the journey I had made in Russian Turkestan…[I] had assisted in the search for camels that strayed while grazing. I knew the silence at night, when one's eyes are burning after marching against the wind all day. I loved the primitive way of living which gave one back that hunger that transforms every morsel one puts under one's tooth into solid satisfaction. (*Forbidden Journey* 88)]

Maillart's narrative and the accompanying photos[7] embrace the monotony of the daily routine as well as the excitement of new discovery. Maillart revels in her surroundings and the people and cultures she encounters. Her detailed descriptions of the indigenous nomads read much like a photograph, providing a clear, visual image for the reader. Her observations of the Other, particularly of women, give witness to a perspective that remains absent from Fleming's narrative. She watches women from all social classes, including princesses (54) and poorer women, admiring their tenacity under difficult circumstances. She maintains an outlook that contrasts markedly with that of her traveling companion:

> Une jeune mère leste et décidée s'est jointe à notre caravane peu après le départ de Bach Malgan; son bébé pleure souvent la nuit, ou vomit, bref "fait tout ce que font ces chères petites choses" comme dit Peter, quelque peu agacé. Mon compagnon va jusqu'à prédire toutes sortes de contretemps: il n'aime pas les femmes, qu'il faut toujours aider, dit-il…Pourtant en voyant ce petit enfant ficelé sur cet âne qui le secoue,

Peter finit par remarquer: "Pauvre gosse!...Il n'a pas la vie drôle!"
Quant à moi je réserve plutôt ma compassion pour la mère. (141)

[A decided-looking and heavily-laden young mother joined our caravan
a little way out from Bash Malghun. Her baby was given to crying at
night and to vomiting; in short, "did all that the dear little things do."
Thus the somewhat peeved Peter. He went so far as to predict all sorts
of difficulties. He did not like women. "You have to be always helping
them," he said...However, as he looked at the child, tied on the donkey
and getting shaken, Peter finished by observing: "Poor little chap! He
hasn't much of a life." My compassion, on the other hand, went out
rather to the mother. (*Forbidden Journey* 173)]

Maillart goes on to describe the rudiments of daily life for most
women in the caravan, from gathering combustibles for the fire to the
careful mixing of *tsamba*, the daily ration of barley, butter, and tea.
While she does not speak the same language, Maillart nonetheless
makes an effort to communicate with the women she encounters
through the help of interpreters or sometimes simply with gestures.
Furthermore, her descriptions of these women do not insist upon her
own western superiority: "La femme du Mir...est une femme
charmante drapée dans une robe de panne grise...Son maintien noble
est plein d'aisance et c'est moi qui suis intimidée quand elle
m'observe de son oeil vif" (227). [The Mir's wife...was a charming
woman dressed in a grey robe of panne velvet...She was very
beautiful, with a distinguished carriage and an air of ease and good
breeding. It was I who felt timid when she looked at me with her
bright eyes (*Forbidden Journey* 290–1).] In fact, Maillart recognizes her
own position as inferior to some of the women she meets. The interest
and the passion that Maillart exhibits for those she meets contrasts
starkly with Fleming's marked indifference. Like Fleming, Maillart
brings with her a preconceived notion of the exotic and the Other—
she gives, for example, necklaces made of red plastic beads to the
women she meets en route (96)—and she cannot completely liberate
herself from a learned, colonial mentality. Nevertheless, Maillart
redirects the colonial gaze by embracing the authenticity of nomadic
life and accepting the Other as her equal. She does not express a need
to dominate or civilize the people she encounters. Instead, she writes
them into her narrative, informing her reader of alternatives to an
occidental perspective.

As for her appreciation of Fleming, Maillart does not hide her disappointment in spite of the camaraderie that he extends to her. Fundamentally, he represents the Europe that she wishes to leave behind, at least for the duration of the journey:

> Mais surtout un morceau d'Europe, matière isolante, nous accompagnait inévitablement par le seul fait de notre communauté ; je n'étais plus à des milliers de kilomètres de tout ce que je connaissais, submergée par une Asie à laquelle je m'intégrais. (47)

> [Above all, a piece of Europe inevitably accompanied us through the mere fact of our association. That isolated us. I was no longer thousands of miles from my own world. I was not submerged by, or integrated into, Asia. (*Forbidden Journey* 46)]

They envision the voyage from two disparate perspectives. If Fleming divides his world according to the traditional colonial paradigm, Maillart works to revise it. She leaves the Occident with the hope of immersing herself in central Asia and its traditions. Her observations of women and nomads highlight another aspect of the journey. Moreover, her total devotion to the voyage distances her from longstanding models of domesticity and femininity. Maillart thus creates an alternative and feminist itinerary for her travel narrative.

Maillart's feminist alternative becomes especially significant in the context of this comparison. An analysis of these two travelogues shows that Fleming's perspective reinforces the colonial gaze whereas Maillart begins to redirect it. In this context, the traveler's vision is thus clearly gender related. For these two writers, the construction of self and the Other is based on fundamentally different understandings of the role of the dominant culture and its relationship to the indigenous one. This stereoscopic vision allows the reader added insight into the voyage, thus creating a third version of this singular trip, a version born of two diverse interpretations. Finally, in order to be able to understand this voyage from Peking to Kashmir, the reader should consider Maillart and Fleming's travel narratives in tandem, for together they provide a multidimensional vision of China and the colonial world in 1935.

Notes

1   I will refer to the geographic names used by Fleming and Maillart in their texts for consistency.

2   In a letter written in May 1994, Ella Maillart wrote to me of her wish to become an ethnographer.

3   For detailed discussions of the role of gender in travel, see, for example, Sarah Mills' *Discourses of Difference: An Analysis of Women's Travel Writing and Colonialism*, Mary Louise Pratt's *Imperial eyes: Travel Writing and Transculturation*, Inderpal Grewal's *Home and Harem: Nation, Gender, Empire, and the Cultures of Travel*, and Sidonie Smith's *Moving Lives: Twentieth-Century Women's Travel Writing*.

4   See chapter one for a discussion of Paul Fussell's *Abroad: British Traveling Between the Wars*.

5   A *lis* is about seven hundred yards.

6   Fleming refers to Maillart as Kini at regular intervals in his narrative. His use of this diminutive further serves to assert his masculine authority.

7   The original version of *Oasis interdites*, published in Paris by Grasset in 1937, included numerous photos from the trip across China as did the edition published by *24 heures* in Lausanne in 1982. The most recent edition of *Oasis interdites*, reprinted in the Voyageurs series by Payot in 1989, contains no photos, despite the author's objections.

Chapter Five

Driving in a Ford:
Two Women Across Afghanistan

Ella Maillart's *The Cruel Way* (1947)[1] chronicles her journey from Switzerland to Afghanistan in the company of writer, poet, and fellow traveler Annemarie Schwarzenbach. The two drive from Geneva to Kabul in a brand new Ford in 1939, on the eve of the Second World War. These two women embark on a trip of some 7782 kilometers that takes them on roads rarely traveled. [2] The voyage, both literally and metaphorically, proves to be one of change and transition. Nothing will be the same again after their arrival in Kabul. This chapter will explore the trials and tribulations of *The Cruel Way*, paying special attention to the various transformations that characterize the voyage. In particular, we will follow the move toward the inner journey for both Maillart and Schwarzenbach, as well as the change in perspective triggered by two women traveling by car. Both gender and mode of transport will thus play critical roles in this analysis. Likewise, historically, change is at hand and will provide unavoidable consequences for the two writers. Finally, this chapter will discuss a fundamental shift in narrative form, one that signals the end of an era and perhaps the beginning of a new one for travel literature in the 20th century.

Maillart's *The Cruel Way* represents a key text in her body of travel narratives for several reasons. First, it signals the move from travel for travel's sake to the inner journey, the ever elusive search for self. This change, at least in part, is dictated by Maillart's traveling companion, Annemarie Schwarzenbach, revealed as the troubled Christina in the text. Obsessed by drugs and her own suffering, the younger Christina occupies Maillart's thoughts and attention en route. As a result, *The Cruel Way* vacillates between observations of places and peoples encountered, characteristic of her prior travel narratives, and reflections on the tortured Christina and Maillart's ability, or inability, to help her. Consider Mary Russell's comments in the introduction to the Beacon Press edition of *The Cruel Way*:

> Once you embark upon *The Cruel Way* you will find there is no going back—you travel at Maillart's speed and at her bidding. The sand will burn your feet and the whistling wind will sting your face. Ahead of you, disappearing into time, you will catch a glimpse of the shadowy caravans of Genghis Khan, Marco Polo and Ibn Batuta for you to follow in their footsteps. And all the time you will hear Ella talking, bullying, cajoling—never ceasing in her efforts to awaken in Christina a perception of Now, the Eternal Present. (xvi)

As Russell suggests, *The Cruel Way* has the reader advance along the path of the traditional travelogue while at the same time introducing a parallel track, the bumpy road that is the relationship between the cajoling Ella Maillart and her struggling traveling companion.

In fact, much of the travelogue is devoted to the evolving notion of self and world for the two women travelers. *The Cruel Way* presents a new set of goals for Maillart, goals that focus on her ability to learn more about herself and, in the process, to share what she learns with Christina in an effort to save her from her struggle with drugs and self-destruction. Maillart's intentions are not entirely altruistic. She hopes to learn from Christina and her suffering. Furthermore, Maillart recognizes the greatness that Christina has to offer the world both as a poet and an author. This desire to find the inner, unnamable self is articulated by Maillart prior to the outset of their journey:

> I uttered a silent prayer: May it be in my power to help you, impatient Christina so irked by the limitations of the human condition, so oppressed by the falsity of life, by the parody of love around us. If we travel together, may it be given me not to fail you, may my shoulder be firm enough for you to lean on. Along the surface of the earth I shall find our way where I have journeyed before; and inwardly, where I have long ago begun to ask myself questions so like yours, may the little that I found help you to find what each of us has to find by himself. (5)

Maillart's silent prayer remains, however, steeped in her usual self-confidence. Assured that she will succeed where others have failed, Maillart makes it her mission to convince Christina to give up morphine and drugs. Her firm determination becomes apparent during their pre-departure preparations and a visit with their mutual friend, Irene:

> During these London days I was staying with Irene who had met Christina at Teheran in 1935. She thought I was unwise to start with such a companion—predicted that we would reach neither Kabul nor Iran. Assuring her she was wrong, I tried to convince her that I knew the "Fallen Angel" better than she. Deep in my heart was an unshakable confidence in Christina and that my double aim—Kabul and helping her—would be attained. (9)

Maillart's wishes to learn about self and save Christina coincide with her impatience with the current reality of living in pre-war Switzerland. Disappointed and disillusioned by Europe's failure to maintain peace after the First World War, Maillart turns eastward, seeking a peaceful alternative to a Europe on the brink of destruction. Throughout the narrative, Maillart questions their abandonment of Europe at this crucial time: what can these two young women offer the war effort? Is there anything to be done? What can they learn from more "primitive" cultures in order to avoid the pitfalls that plague the west? Such questions propel the narrative as Maillart and Christina literally leave Europe behind them.

Before considering how the two travelers fare together, we should examine what Annemarie Schwarzenbach brings to their shared adventure. Poet, photographer, and traveler, Annemarie Schwarzenbach undoubtedly enjoys greater literary fame today than her traveling companion. For her part, Schwarzenbach devoted a series of essays to this same journey, some published in newspapers or magazines, others compiled later from unpublished manuscripts. Nine essays on Afghanistan, seven of which were written during or about her travels with Maillart, appear in the posthumous collection *Auf der Schattenseit* (1990). In 2000, Lenos Verlag published *Alle Wege sind offen: Die Reise nach Afghanistan 1939–1940*, a collection of previously published newspaper articles about their travels to Afghanistan.[3] Prior to their voyage in her Ford, Schwarzenbach had already traveled extensively in the Near East, the United States, and Europe, thus bringing her own wealth of experiences to their combined endeavour. These ex-

periences, however, mixed brilliance and tragedy: the young
Schwarzenbach finished her doctorate and published her first novel
by the age of twenty-three (Linsmayer 134).[4] Frequent companion of
Erika and Klaus Mann, Barbara Wright and Carson McCullers,
Annemarie Schwarzenbach seemed to have all an aspiring writer
could desire: influential friends, talent, inspiration, and family wealth
behind her. Yet Annemarie Schwarzenbach remained somehow in-
consolable, always searching. As Charles Linsmayer explains in his
biographical afterward to Schwarzenbach's most renowned novel,
Das Glückliche Tal, translated into French as *La Vallée heureuse*: "Cette
séduisante jeune fille d'un excellent milieu faisait de plus en plus
parler de sa famille à cause de ses amours scandaleuses et même, plus
tard, à cause d'histoires d'abus d'alcool, de consommation de drogue
et de tentatives de suicide!" (147). [This seductive young woman from
an excellent milieu caused people to talk about her family first due to
her scandalous love affairs and later due to the stories of alcohol and
drug abuse as well as repeated suicide attempts.] By the time
Schwarzenbach traveled to Afghanistan with Ella Maillart in 1939, she
had endured numerous failed love affairs with members of both
sexes, had married and divorced French diplomat Claude Clarac, and
had been in and out of detoxification clinics in and effort to cure her
drug abuse. Travel with Maillart undoubtedly offered Schwarzenbach
a welcomed escape, an opportunity to leave behind long-standing
family conflicts, including a problematic relationship with her
mother, and the war brewing in Europe.

As such, Christina's goals and desires seem to mesh well with
Maillart's as the two prepare their departure. Like Maillart, Christina
seeks an alternative to war, and as she notes in her essay "La
Steppe",[5] the seductive image of travel might seem like a palatable
possibility:

> Mais le voyage, qui peut paraître à beaucoup comme un rêve léger,
> comme un jeu séduisant, comme une façon de se libérer du quotidien,
> comme la liberté par excellence, est en réalité impitoyable ; c'est une
> école susceptible de nous accoutumer à l'inévitable cours des choses,
> aux rencontres et aux séparations, sans le moindre ménagement. (45)

> [But the voyage, which might seem to many like an easy dream, a se-
> ductive game, a way to liberate oneself from the daily routine, the ulti-
> mate freedom, is in reality unforgiving: it is a school likely to get us

[used to the inevitable way things work, to unceremonious meetings and separations.]

Ultimately, Schwarzenbach will find it impossible to turn her back on Europe and will make her way back there to join in the fight against Hitler. Before her return, however, Christina recognizes the need to concentrate fully on her more personal battle with drug use. She considers her need to free herself from morphine to be the motivating force behind their journey. She looks to Maillart for the strength she seems to lack, as Maillart writes in *The Cruel Way*:

> I [Christina] am thirty. It is the last chance to mend my ways, to take myself in hand. This journey is not going to be a sky-larking escapade as if we were twenty—and that is impossible, with the European crisis increasing day by day. This journey must be a means towards our end. We can help each other to become conscious, responsible persons. My blind way of life has grown unbearable. What is the reason, the meaning of the chaos that undermines people and nations? And there must be something that I am to do with my life, there must be some purpose for which I could gladly die or live! Kini...how do you live? (4)

Until now, drugs have been Christina's route to self-understanding and to self-destruction, a means to forget the reality at hand. By mending her ways, she hopes to leave drugs and the inevitable cures that follow behind her, exhausted by clinics, doctors, and her own family.[6] She, like Maillart, seeks to give meaning to her life. She hopes that Maillart, older, stable, and more experienced, can help her find the purpose that seems to elude her.

Both Schwarzenbach and Maillart leave Europe with certain romantic dreams of self realization intact. Sidonie Smith describes a similar desire when analyzing Robyn Davison's 1971 trip across the Australian outback by camel: "Davison participates in certain historical practices through which white westerners have constituted 'Aboriginality' as radical difference, a radical difference whose curative powers can deliver an enervated westerner to a 'truer' more satisfying experience of self" (*Moving Lives* 66). For the two Swiss traveling together, the Afghani nomads replace the Aboriginals of whom Smith speaks. Like Davison who traveled after them, and like Alexandra David-Néel and Isabella Eberhard who traveled before them, Maillart and Schwarzenbach seek to know themselves better in part thanks to their encounters with radical difference. Because the two have traveled extensively prior to this journey, this phenomenon is hardly new to them. As Smith explains about women travelers in general:

> Released into the vast exteriority of a different landscape, they seek a new interiority of agency forged through the arduous process of cross-cultural identification. Requisite to this interiorization of agency is the identification with subjects of radical difference...subjects assigned an intimate connection with space rather than time (history), subjects imagined as living our more "pure" or "true" or "heroic" or "meaningful" lives than the masses of people ensnared in an enervated modernity. (*Moving Lives* 68)

In contrast with Alexandra David-Néel and Isabella Eberhard, Maillart and Schwarzenbach do not cloak themselves in local garb in an effort to blend in with the indigenous culture during their travels from Switzerland to Afghanistan. They do, however, intend to use their encounters with Afghani nomads and women to enlighten their own understanding of the world and themselves. As Sidonie Smith suggests, they seek truth away from modernity, and specifically away from a Europe bent on aggression. Unlike the more solitary women travelers who figure in chapter two of Smith's study[7], Maillart and Schwarzenbach also have each other. While neither embodies the radical otherness offered by those people they meet on the road to Afghanistan, their very different perspectives on self, the war, and engagement will provide yet another example of radical difference.

Both have tacitly agreed to leave behind western notions of domesticity and femininity as they drive toward the wild, unknown and hence decidedly unfeminine space of central Afghanistan. For Schwarzenbach, notions of gender, femininity, and masculinity figure prominently in her search for self-understanding. The idea of forsaking Europe and the scripted gender roles that constrain her must appeal to Schwarzenbach. Having experimented at length with drugs, failed at marriage, and acknowledged her bisexuality, Schwarzenbach no longer fits well into the bourgeois, Zurich society to which her family belongs. Afghanistan, undoubtedly no less rigid in assigning cultural gender roles, nonetheless represents the romantic unknown, hence a space where she may reinvent herself. Schwarzenbach embarks on their voyage dressed boyishly, evoking a very androgynous notion of self. As Maillart observes en route: "Christina was also in a gay mood: the paymaster had addressed her as Monsieur! The further we moved eastward, the more often she was taken for a boy" (36).

Christina clearly relishes the blurring of gender lines. Through this cultivated androgyny, she will work to come to terms with her own sexuality.

Maillart, on the other hand, sees little romance in her companion's androgynous look and dress. Knowing that in order to observe Afghani women, two women would travel with greater ease than a woman in the company of a man or a boy, Maillart persuades her companion to add a skirt to her wardrobe: "I had convinced her that as long as she wore her grey bags she would be taken for a man and Afghan harems would remain closed to her. I was also convinced that when difficulties are encountered in Asia, women are more readily helped if they are seen to be without a man" (98). Maillart thus favors her female identity as a means to have access to otherwise closed societies. Furthermore, her indomitable spirit of pragmatism undoubtedly clashes with her companion's more romantic vision of self and suffering. The dominating force of her eminent practicality may explain, at least in part, why Maillart never elaborates at length on her own sexuality in her writing: clearly, for Maillart, sexuality remains secondary in her understanding of self and Other.

Christina professes her own internal suffering related to love, and Maillart, in turn, rationalizes and works to explain logically the sentiments of her traveling companion:

> On our way to Maimeneh we discussed a subject about which neither of us knew anything. I had noticed how often Christina's eyes had rested upon the handsome daughter-in-law. And now Christina asked if I thought it was perverse of her to be profoundly moved by the charm of a woman. (144)

Maillart begins by citing her ignorance on the subject, matched by the ignorance of Christina. She then formulates a fundamental question on lesbian identity and bisexuality, one that is never really answered in the course of her book. She recognizes, however, the importance of the response for Christina: "It was a delicate question to answer, for it had roots and branches in every part of Christina's life" (144). Maillart would prefer to avoid the question altogether, but realizes that "It would not be enough for me to tell Christina that she was the most straight and honest person I have met" (144). Word choice indicates Maillart's latent desire to move Christina into the realm of the straight, hence heterosexual.

The paragraph that follows offers perhaps the longest discussion of sexuality that Maillart undertakes in any of her travel narratives, and hence demands a closer look. Maillart begins by separating her experience from that of her companion. She goes on to explain why she would even take the time to discuss the subject of sexuality here in a book devoted to their travels: "But my range of experience being quite different from hers, I could not analyse the cause of her reactions. When we had cross-questioned each other and talked at leisure, we reached certain conclusions which I reproduce here briefly because we have been so interested by them" (144). Hence, lesbian sexuality or what we might call today transexuality becomes a topic worthy of discussion in the book only in so much as it helped produce lengthy discussion along the way. The discussion that Maillart chooses to provide for the reader remains sterile, almost clinical in its description, and utterly lacking in emotion or sentiment:

> For those who identify themselves completely with their bodies, it would be deplorable if they were to be mainly attracted by the qualities of their own sex. Physiological laws being by-passed, unfulfilment (sic) would be a first penalty followed by such mental consequences as morbidity and lack of balance. (144)

Thus, Maillart initially condemns lesbian relationships and homosexual relationships in general, citing a list of undesirable consequences. She goes on, however, to qualify her remarks for those she calls "exceptional" individuals:

> But with exceptional people who identify themselves almost entirely with their mind, who know that thought is foremost because where there is no thought there can be neither body nor object, the question is less important: the mind has no sex, or rather, it comprises both sexes alternately or even simultaneously. The body may grumble now and then at being forgotten, but since it is conditioned by the mind of which it is only a temporary tool, it will be unable to upset that mind. (144)

In examining this paragraph, it is especially important to consider the spiritual and intellectual context in which the author finds herself as she writes *The Cruel Way*. After completing the drive to Afghanistan, Maillart does not return to Europe. Instead, she travels to southern India, where she spends the next five years learning from the Indian sage Ramana Maharishi. The influence of her time spent in the company of Sri Ramana resonates in the prose she writes here:

"the mind has no sex, or rather, it comprises both sexes alternately or even simultaneously" (144). This particular idea, one that negates a western binary division of hetero- and homosexual, helps Maillart to navigate both Schwarzenbach's understanding of sexuality and their particular relationship. According to Maillart, her companion remains an individual to whom the constraints of hetero- or homosexuality do not apply: "For such people it cannot be of grave consequence if they disobey the laws of nature: they can be said to have transcended them" (144). Had Christina truly transcended the laws of nature, the sight of another woman would not provoke a troubling reaction. As Maillart observes, however, Christina falters between desire and intellect:

> But there is trouble ahead for those who are at one moment centred in the mind, the next in the body: the liberty the mind enjoyed is challenged, then, by natural laws that claim supremacy as soon as the body is given pre-eminence. No plane of being, in consequence, can learn its lesson: there is no way of coming to a conclusion or of finding a consistent line of action that could lead to peace. Unwillingly, unknowingly, people find themselves trying to ride two proud horses at the same time—the stallion Nature and the hermaphrodite Mind. They suffer, then, from being torn apart. As Christina was torn, perhaps. (144–5)

According to Maillart, Christina remains mired in this divide, unable to reconcile mind and body. One cannot help thinking that Maillart's analysis fits her own situation better than her companion's. After all, Schwarzenbach has clearly rejected heterosexuality, and suffers a series of failures in her relationships with other women.[8] Despite these failures, she openly embraces lesbianism and bisexuality, living precociously in the 1930s and early 1940s what we might today refer to as a transgendered lifestyle. For Schwarzenbach, mind and body seem to remain, in fact, indivisible.

Maillart, on the other hand, wrestles quietly with the schism that she attributes to her companion. Interestingly enough, she assigns nature the male role of the stallion while according the mind the role of hermaphrodite. Clearly, she uses these metaphors to refer to the perceived split between body and mind. But a closer look at her word choice shows a transformation of female Mother Nature into a male breed. Nature thus no longer represents birth and rejuvenation but raw strength and speed. The power generated by the image of the stallion perhaps coincides with Maillart's own valorization of physical strength, as seen in her own athletic physique and indomitable persona. It also offers a ready contrast to the frail, chain-smoking picture painted of Schwarzenbach. Maillart posits the image of the wild, virile stallion against that of the mind, characterized as gender-less and androgynous; at once asexual and both sexes united. Throughout her discourse, it appears that Maillart seeks to attain the realm of the mind, one free from the constraints and desires of the (masculine) body. Or perhaps more accurately, she seeks to attain unity of mind and body, a unity found in the teachings of the east, in her hermaphrodite conception of mind. The discussion of her companion's sexuality leads the reader to imagine that while Christina suffers endlessly, Maillart may be the one still torn between conflicting identities, despite her efforts to transcend them.

It is difficult to elaborate further on Maillart's discussion of sexuality because the text abruptly abandons the subject, literally traveling farther along the road of their journey. As was the case in her voyage across China with Peter Fleming, Maillart only makes brief references to her rapport with her traveling companion and to the tensions that arose between them in *The Cruel Way*. Nonetheless, these references coupled with the author's preoccupation with Christina's well being become significant markers of the text's move toward an analysis of the inner, spiritual journey. Maillart even broaches the question of love for her companion, but only after their arrival in Afghanistan. Here, she makes clear her strictly platonic intentions, refusing to acknowledge any ulterior sentiment. When Christina comments that she cannot understand how Maillart can love her, Maillart replies: "Christina, I don't know myself. How can I answer? But I think I now see very clearly something great in you. Is it perhaps what people mean when they say they love someone 'in God'?" (201). Unwilling to consider the possibility of any other love for Christina, Maillart carefully sidesteps the question of her own sexuality. Her total avoidance of the question of a sexual relationship between her traveling companion and herself reflects a silence on this subject characteristic of her travel narratives and her life in general. While she readily adapts a life of travel in order to avoid certain stereotypes of femininity and domesticity, she shows no interest in establishing an alternative to the dominant heterosexual paradigm in lesbianism or bisexuality. On the contrary, as noted in earlier citations and in her writings and letters from India,[9] she somewhat awkwardly articulates her understanding of sexuality according to alternative models of self and gender, models not founded on the division of body and spirit, of masculine and feminine.

Traditional notions of masculinity and femininity are further confounded in Maillart's narrative when we turn to the role of the car and automobile travel. As Sidonie Smith explains: "women used automobiles as vehicles of resistance to conventional gender roles and the strictures of a normative femininity. Autos provided access...to recreational travel" (175). The automobile thus provides Maillart and Schwarzenbach with the freedom of movement to undertake their journey in the spirit of resistance mentioned here. At the same time, the car carries certain implications that might undermine this resistance, particularly when one considers the car as a feminized possession, one that characterizes the male domain. Men drive cars that become their sweethearts, their babies. They exert power over this treasured possession. As Smith observes: "Far more than any other form of transportation, the automobile has been associated with male sexual prowess...In the imagination, the automobile itself is bisexual. Men often imagine their cars as female; they are possessions. But they also imagine them as prosthetic extensions of the sexual organ. They are, in this sense, possessed of phallic power" (183). This bisexual configuration of the automobile proves especially useful in our analysis of Maillart and Schwarzenbach's trip across Afghanistan. For, in their case, the car may indeed be read as both masculine and feminine. The androgynous Schwarzenbach, cloaked in male clothing, literally becomes the boy driving the car for most of the journey. Driving asserts Schwarzenbach's control, her ability to be independent and in charge, qualities that are otherwise brought into question by her repeated relapses into drugs. Driving provides a certain power to Schwarzenbach that eludes Maillart and helps assure a more balanced relationship between the two. Maillart rides alongside—stronger, more stable, older—but unable to master the clutch along steep grades of road. She, however, hardly incarnates the typical image of a girl riding alongside in the front seat of a car. On the contrary, both Maillart and Schwarzenbach are empowered by the freedom of movement that the car accords them. No longer confined to buses prone to breaking down and the pre-determined stops they make (as Maillart was on her first trip through Iran a couple of years earlier),[10] the two travelers can literally be the first to cover many stretches of the newly laid road. As Smith notes:

> Not confined by schedules, tracks, and prepackaged destinations, the traveler, with hands on the wheel, can change the course, speed, and rhythm of encounter and perspective. Nestled inside the cab, the auto-mobilist thus experiences an insular, autonomous individuality and an exhilarating freedom of movement. (170)

Maillart and Schwarzenbach undoubtedly share this experience of freedom of motion, but the car seems to assure their identity as Euro-peans, rather than as autonomous individuals, the farther east they travel. What constitutes their individuality, perhaps even a novelty to local spectators, is the fact that two women arrive in the car. The car thus represents their mode of escape—from gender roles, from a Europe in crisis—as well as their arrival at a new definition of self, one confronted directly with the foreign Other. The car brings Maillart and Schwarzenbach into contact with new people and new places. Their travel along the road gives them the opportunity to wit-ness and criticize colonial influence along the way. Such criticism will serve to help them understand better this encounter with the Other and their ever-evolving perception of self.

The car provides a different perspective than travel by horseback or camel, by foot or by train. In her previous experiences, Maillart's encounters with indigenous cultures and peoples seemed less intru-sive, in part because she traveled much as they did.[11] If the car high-lights the differences between traditional cultures and modernity, it also allows Maillart and Schwarzenbach to drive straight into the lives of their fellow Europeans. A mechanized passport, the car as-sures that they will be received by fellow "moderns" all along the way. In these encounters, typically with engineers actually responsi-ble for building the new roads or capitalists in charge of factories and new economic development, Maillart reveals a critical eye for her fel-low Europeans. Her travel experience in Asia provides her with an acute understanding of the colonial endeavour, one that posits the Europeans as superior simply out of principle:

> But I have often noticed that Westerners have an inborn tendency to minimise or ridicule whatever the Persians do—not because it is badly done, but simply because they are exasperated by the pride of the Per-sian who boasts that what he has done is "the best in the world". They

do not see that among Asiatics this attitude is the inevitable reaction to the condescension with which Westerners brought their mechanical progress to the East as if it were a revealed religion capable of healing all ills. (69)

Her reading of colonialism as a sort of religion imposed upon Asia seems remarkably accurate, especially in light of today's post-colonial context. Maillart understands better than most the importance of local customs, culture, and religious practices. As such, she is quick to criticize the director of a factory and his wife, who cannot understand why she and a friend cannot bathe in plain sight in the local river. After all, they wear western bathing suits. Maillart repeats the words of Frau Kuhn, clearly pointing to the religious and cultural divide that separates Afghanis from the German engineers:

Anyhow, Herr Kuhn made it clear to the Elder of the valley that the two khanums [unaccompanied women] would go on bathing. He would submit to the laws of the country most willingly, but he was going to live according to the customs of Germany. He was not prepared to hide his wife under a shroud every time she came out of the house. (160)

Unfortunately, the speaker fails to see the irony of the situation, unable to understand why cultural differences might be even more dangerous than legal ones. She sees no reason to accommodate a culture other than her own.

Maillart, on the other hand, mocks the innate sense of superiority that characterizes the Germans' speech. Clearly, for Maillart, this is more than a personal misunderstanding, but rather symptomatic of the fundamental problems inherent in the entire European colonial endeavour:

Men must certainly be fed and clothed, but in doing this must strangle their most important faculties? In other words: Is it necessary that each Asiatic country should go to the bitter end of our materialistic experiment? Taking it for granted that Europe is now beginning to see the need of founding its life once more in spiritual values, when will Asia in its turn see through the mirage of "immediate industrialisation at all costs"?...They will be unable to fight the moral depression that crawls in the wake of our materialistic culture. Mines, oil, electricity, coal, offer quick and big returns. Cattle, fruit, lambskins, wool, wheat, forests, demand patience but they are Afghan products calling for Afghan activities: they provoke no rupture with the past, no forcing of an alien growth. (163)

Maillart's analysis dispenses with the typical defenses of colonialism—that it provides education, medical care, and raises the standard of living—and points to the inherent dangers threatening indigenous cultures:

> Our Western ideas will spread further with the development of education. It will help to make a young man more quickly free on the material plane: he will no longer need to obey Gholam Haidar, his father-in-law, or whoever was keeping him. But our kind of education is a dangerous solvent: it divides, it will teach him to criticize, he will think he knows enough to judge. (164)

She goes onto attack Soviet colonialism, an expansionism embarked upon in the name of the people, one that she has observed first hand in her travels. As Maillart observes, even the advancement of the proletariat comes at the price of an entire culture:

> The question is: are advantages of hospital, school, newspaper or wireless at the disposal of the new factory-hand, worth the loss of the lingering smile that use to accompany his hard but well-balanced life? Soviet Russia answers: Yes, because the profits made by the factory don't go to a Shah or a plutocrat but ultimately return to the worker. I say No, convinced that if you spend the best part of your energy walking two steps one way, then two steps the other way eight hours a day year after year, mending the broken threads of devilish spinning bobbins, you have no inspiration or vitality left for living your own life during the rest of the day. (164)

Maillart's sharp, direct criticism of the colonial endeavor signals a maturing and evolving perspective, one that contrasts with the prose of her first travel narrative, *Parmi la jeunesse russe*, characterized by its enthusiasm for Soviet ingenuity. Since that time, Maillart has gradually come to recognize the inevitable effects of colonial expansion, be it Soviet or otherwise, on indigenous and nomadic cultures in Soviet Turkistan, China, Iran, and finally Afghanistan.

Maillart's criticism of colonialism in Afghanistan is well-founded. Afghanistan, like many of its neighbors in Asia, wrestled with European colonialism for the better part of a century. The First Anglo-Afghan war in 1839 resulted in the installation of a puppet king by the British and a continued struggle for freedom by the Afghans. By 1843, the Afghani people had ousted British rule, but two more Anglo-Afghan wars followed in 1878 and 1921. To the north, Afghani relations with Russia followed a similar path. Russia seized Afghani territory in 1885, but later agreed to recognize Afghani sovereignty, thus assuring close but increasingly problematic relations between the two states. Maillart's travels are marked by the progressive reforms and the subsequent reactions that came following the third Anglo-Afghan War in 1921. At that time, in an effort to modernize and westernize Aghanistan as quickly as possible, "Amanullah Khan initiates a series of ambitious efforts at social and political modernization" (*Afghanistan Online*). By the 1930s, Amanullah Khan had been removed from power and his reforms abolished by his successor. We see Ella Maillart reacting to these changes and to the strong German presence in Afghanistan at the time in her travelogue.

Despite her criticism, Maillart's itinerate travel is, nonetheless, inexorably linked to colonial expansion, to roads and rail laid in the name of progress and the state. As such, a certain aura of discovery accompanies the two travelers as they drive across roads rarely frequented. They remain a novelty at every border crossing, as Maillart remarks: "At the Persian post, a sort of great school-hall, we feared we should not be allowed to travel further. Though it vexed him, the official had to admit he did not know what to do with a *tryptique* and *carnet de passage*. So Christina filled up all the entries in his book. We saw that we were car number two entering Iran by this road" (56). Maillart and Christina clearly relish the potential road blocks and dangers associated with the voyage. Likewise, they enjoy the knowledge that they are only the second car of record to pass through the borders. Their delight, however, is later tempered by sobering observations of the changes instigated by the creation of borders where there once were none: "Here, where thousands and thousands of sheep, horses and camels used to roam, not a sign of life was to be seen. Nomads and their ways of life belonged to the past. Even if we had gone further afield towards Bujnurd, we should have seen none of the once famous Turkoman horse-breeders: they are no more" (91).

Maillart's observations concerning the nomadic people of the region stem from an infatuation that has lasted most of her adult life. This affiliation between the nomad, woman traveler and nomadic tribes is perhaps no coincidence. As Deborah Paes de Barros explains in *Fast Cars and Bad Girls. Nomadic Subjects and Women's Road Stories*:

> Resistance to hegemonic and patriarchal discourse marks both feminist and nomadic consciousness. Nomadism reflects a kind of constructed

> subjectivity—a subjectivity that is consistent with certain aspects of feminist discourse(s). But, if women are often affiliated with the nomadic sensibility through a certain shared subjectivity, the woman traveler—the literal woman nomad who ventures the reality of the road—frequently forms a profound relationship with the notion of the nomad. (10)

Although Paes de Barros addresses American literature in her study, her remarks apply especially well to the traveling Maillart, whose desire to evade Europe and the confines of western living has been accompanied by an equally strong desire to rejoin what she calls a more authentic way of life, exemplified by the nomads of central Asia. Gilles Deleuze and Felix Guattari have theorized extensively on the concept of the nomad,[12] and Rosi Braidotti proposes an eloquent and convincing theory of the nomadic subject and feminism, one that she links specifically to the post-modern.[13] Maillart, however, does not yet belong to this post-modern world. She remains poised on the brink of post-modernism, writing from India in the 1940s, one of the last fortresses of a crumbling British colonialism. If, as Paes de Barros suggests, Maillart identifies with the constructed subjectivity of the nomad, she does not define herself according to the many fragments and pieces of post-modern identities. Her identification with nomadic peoples is not metaphoric but literal, and by the time she writes *The Cruel Way* Maillart understands that she will never be able to realize her dream of living among nomads.

Nonetheless, this long-term identification has made her acutely aware of the their plight. Conscious of the effects of the modern nation state, Maillart astutely predicts the demise of nomadic cultures in the face of modernity:

> Nomadic life is doomed even in Saudi Arabia or in Mongolia, and I think the main reasons for this disappearance are the same in all these countries. Nowadays frontiers are exactly delimited and they complicate nomadic life. The central power of every country wants to become strong, needs obedient soldiers and settled tax-paying subjects; to make his country independent, the Chief of State has to enforce these conditions at all costs; that this kind of independence is not the one wanted by nomads cannot be taken into consideration. People who obey only their tribal laws cannot be allowed in modern states. (181)

Her description of the fate of the world's nomadic population rings prophetic in light of the realities of the early 21st century, in particular the plight of the Kurds and the Kirghiz, some sixty-five years after her travels to Afghanistan:

> Because they [nomads] are fully themselves, they can only with diffi-
> culty become peasants or artisans; not having known the old life, their
> children may be more adaptable. In the meantime, this wonderful hu-
> man material is wasted. The Kurds are in utter misery, their ways of
> living crushed, whether in Turkey, Iran or Iraq. Other nomads, some
> two hundred thousand of them, were sent away from the mountains of
> South Persia or fled to sun-scorched Mesopotamia where they all died
> within two years. In Turkestan, the Kazak-Kirghizes as well as the
> Turkomans have melted away by the millions. The Mongols had to give
> away their pasture-land to innumerable Chinese settlers supported by
> the authorities. (182)

Maillart points to the irreparable loss of peoples and their cultures with regret and awareness. Her travels will do nothing to bring back the life of the nomad, as Maillart is keenly aware. Hence, the voyage remains bittersweet for Maillart, at once an exercise in freedom and a lesson in subjugation and loss. This duality will characterize both the actual voyage to Afghanistan as well as the inner voyage toward a more clear understanding of self, one that continues to be informed by her identification with nomadic subjectivity.

In fact, Maillart identifies more readily with the figure of the no-mad than with her European traveling companion. Ultimately, travel to Afghanistan in the company of Annemarie Schwarzenbach proves to be one of the most difficult undertakings of Maillart's career. She expresses clearly at the outset of the voyage her desire to save the younger Schwarzenbach, from drugs, suffering, and ultimately self-destruction. The lapse of several years between her trip to Afghanistan and the actual writing of the book helps Maillart recog-nize the extent to which her own ego is wrapped up in her voiced desire to help her companion : "if at the start there was an élan of un-selfishness in my desire to help Christina, it was mixed by now with pride and vanity: I, Kini, could not bear to be beaten—could not, therefore, fail" (27). Indeed, Maillart's quest to liberate her friend from drugs becomes a personal challenge, one that she seems determined to win at all costs. This explains, at least in part, Maillart's pitiless at-titude toward Schwarzenbach and her morphine addition. Maillart fears falling into the same trap of compassion that has ensnared other mutual friends. Maillart thus presents a stern, unforgiving face to the sufferings of Christina, hoping to jolt her out of her helplessness:

> She was probably suffering agonies . . . Even so I should be firm and treat her like a man, showing no emotion or tender weakness that she might use towards her ruin. I wondered if those who helped her before had not been too fond of her, too worried by her misery, too ready to let her have her own way? I hoped to succeed where they had failed because I was different from them, not loving her as they did: this was probably why I had a slight hold on her. (25)

Maillart's decision to treat Schwarzenbach "like a man" echoes her desire to play the male role, to embody masculine strength. She does not choose to nurture Schwarzenbach, but rather to share a sort of tough love, one with no trace of emotion. Only at the end of the journey, obliged to acknowledge Christina's repeated relapses and utter failure to forego morphine, does Maillart recognize her own errors in judgement: "After the Sofia incident I chose to appear hard and determined not to forgive another relapse. So, when the hour of trial came, Christina was naturally afraid of me. I had singled out that line of action imagining that it might be more successful than the tenderness of her former friends" (199). This recognition of personal failure seems to shock Maillart and push her toward a new understanding of both self and Other. She notes somewhat incredulously that

> even when she [Christina] opened her eyes, looked at me from the depth of her helplessness and said she felt like death, I failed to grasp what was happening...But the evidence flashed when I saw on the floor of the bathroom the brittle glass of an empty ampoule. She had succumbed once more. She had disregarded our compact; she had done what she pretended to abhor. My presence, my confidence in her, the fear of displeasing me had had no effect. (24)

Maillart does not realize that her inability to exert any sort of external control over her traveling companion only mirrors her companion's own lack of self-control. This undisciplined approach to life contrasts starkly with Maillart's vision of self and the world. Maillart assumes that an individual will take responsibility for her behavior and actions, an assumption that Schwarzenbach repeatedly rejects with her continued forays into drugs. Ultimately, Maillart sees in Schwarzenbach a radical Otherness with which she can never identify. By the time they reach Kabul, Schwarzenbach seems to have less in common with Maillart than the Afghani nomad women they have encountered along the way. Christina's final confession leaves Maillart utterly disillusioned:

> At last she spoke. A confession of her total wretchedness. She had lied all the time. As soon as the war had shaken our plans, her old demon had raised its head. Her craving for codeine had marked the start. And then once more, the old story: with mad recklessness, with fierce cunning, her second self had found the great number of ampoules she needed.
> But now she was so sick, so far gone, that something drastic must be done. She could not bring herself to follow the declining doses ordered by the German doctor. Once more she had no choice but to adopt the most radical remedy—run away from the town. (199)

Arrival in Kabul thus marks at once success and failure for the two travelers. They have completed the long and arduous drive to Afghanistan, but have done nothing to remedy Schwarzenbach's drug problem. Roger Perret, in his afterward to Schwarzenbach's *Où est la terre des promesses*, confirms that the arrival at their goal is at best bittersweet :

> Désespérée par la guerre, exténuée par la maladie, passionnément amoureuse de Ria Hackin,[14] il lui [Schwarzenbach] fut impossible de résister à la fascination du poison. Ella Maillart vécut cet épisode comme la rupture du pacte conclu avec elle. En meme temps, elle se reprochait d'avoir failli à son role d'ange gardien. (187)

> [Despairing about the war, exhausted by her illness, passionately in love with Ria Hackin, it was impossible for her [Schwarzenbach] to resist the poison's fascination. Ella Maillart considered this episode to be the final rupture of the pact upon which they had agreed. At the same time, she reproached herself for having failed in her role as guardian angel.]

Obliged to acknowledge a stinging disappointment, Maillart somewhat abruptly takes leave of her companion, abandoning her to a mutual friend who will accompany her to northern Afghanistan to join an archeological dig.[15] With some discomfort, Maillart recognizes how she has turned Christina's struggle into her own:

> During all this time in Kabul there lived in me a pin-point of uneasiness which expressed itself months later in the feeling: I failed Christina. According to our pact I was not to leave her alone whatever she might say

or do. But the intensity of my desire to help her had spoiled my intention. That intensity had brought with it a kind of effort that had tired
me. Had goodness been part of me I should have helped her with de-
tachment, quite simply and because I could not do otherwise...I should
not have vitiated the movement by thinking: "*I* must succeed, *I* have to
succeed!" (198).

Maillart will meet with Christina one last time in Central India
early in 1940. Maillart has elected to stay in India, while Christina
prepares her return to Switzerland. Christina chooses to engage in the
fight against Nazism, and encourages Maillart to do the same.[16]
Maillart rejects this possibility in favor of the teachings of the Indian
sages in an effort to find an alternative to war. This final separation
marks Maillart's failure to reach one of her stated goals. It remains for
her to work to fulfill the other, the search for self knowledge.

As Maillart states early on, part of this inner journey has been
masked by her search for nomadic peoples and a more authentic way
of life. Her desire to help Christina is likewise enmeshed in this ongoing quest for self and the Other. As Maillart notes before setting out
on their journey, she knew very well what she intended to accomplish
in the drive across Afghanistan:

> Briefly stated, my main aims were to acquire self-mastery and to save
> my friend from herself. The second aim depended on the first. Only
> clear knowledge of myself would allow me to help Christina in the fun-
> damental problem she was raising. Of course that mastery of myself
> should bring me nearer to reality, and ever since I began roughing it
> among sailors and nomads I was in search of a "real" life. (26)

Maillart reflects on the nature of the goals she has set for herself during the writing process. For the first time, Maillart acknowledges that
her search for authenticity among nomadic tribes stems from her desire to know herself better, to provide an excuse to leave a Europe on
the brink of war: "Away from a shaky and feverish Europe I simply
wanted to look within. My search for an Edenic mountain tribe was
merely the excuse for breaking away from the helplessness prevalent
in Europe" (27).

In point of fact, Maillart and Schwarzenbach encounter few nomads as they motor along the road leading to and through
Afghanistan. While in previous journeys Maillart's observations
gravitated toward the women of the caravans, in Afghanistan women
remain virtually hidden from sight. On the way to a local market, for

example, "men thronged the road at our feet. No trees, nothing but a world of yellow earth and yellow earthen walls in which the white of turbans and the red of kaftans vibrated joyfully as if in a composition by a master-painter. As usual, not a woman to be seen" (141). This phenomenon does not simply arise because women remain hidden from view in Muslim countries. By choosing to travel by car, the symbol of twentieth-century modernity, Maillart and Schwarzenbach can never integrate themselves into Afghanistan's pre-modern landscape. The two travelers benefit from the unrivaled hospitality of the Afghan people, but remain the very foreign Others, especially with regard to other women. As Schwarzenbach notes in her essay entitled "Dans le jardin des belles jeunes filles de Quaisar," Ella's question to a local governor about excluding women and girls from the inevitable progress that will accompany the roads being built in Afghanistan is met with an evasive response at best. When they ask to meet with the governor's wife, the governor agrees initially, only to come up with an excuse to refuse their request shortly thereafter (87–8). Only by chance will they have the opportunity to speak with women of the indigenous Afghani tribes. Wary of breaking down in the middle of the desert, the two travelers nonetheless stop when they hear wailing coming from a black tent : "Interrupting their mourning, the women came out to us, unveiled, unforgettable in dark-red garments under black head-cloths. We inspected, fingered, questioned each other, till a man came along who tried to send our new friends away. We were at once all leagued against him in good humour: outbursts of laughter received my remark that "Women can do well without men!" (*The Cruel Way* 168) This easy collegiality that arises among women seems to confirm that Maillart feels more at ease with those she meets along the way than with her traveling companion. The women of Afghanistan may represent the foreign Other for Maillart, but no one will embody otherness like Schwarzenbach.

This identification of the Other serves Maillart well in her intensified quest for self-knowledge. Convinced after failure to save Christina that the only path left is the one that leads inwards, Maillart uses the writing process to continue that journey. She compares herself to Christina in an effort to understand their relationship, pointing to the commonalities that brought them together in the first place: both sought to earn a living, lived alone, and "deplored the poor quality of love" (75) they could offer others. As Maillart goes on to explain, these similarities cannot bridge the fundamental differences in personality and perspective: "We were both travellers—she always running away from an emotional crisis (not seeing that she was already wishing for the next), I always seeking far afield the secret of harmonious living, or filling up time by courting risk" (75). Likewise, Maillart's pragmatic nature contrasts sharply with Christina's more romantic vision of self and suffering: "Mentally we were very different. She was a poet moving among ideas shaped and enlivened by her imagination, her moods changing the world. Whereas I still believed in the reality of facts as such, thinking the external world responsible for my subjective life" (75–6). Writing *The Cruel Way* allows Maillart to come to terms with these diverse world views, and helps her to understand why her goal to save her friend was probably doomed from the start.

As she defines herself in contrast with the Other, Maillart goes on to speculate on the reasons for this paradigm shift away from observations of their travels and toward the inner journey. As she notes early on: "This giving form to our innermost tendency goes beyond ethics: a time comes when, in spite of everything, we have to be as true as we can, revealing the essence of ourselves" (38). Ostensibly explaining her choice to flee the war in Europe, Maillart reveals perhaps the influence of the time spent in India reflecting on the nature of truth and self. As she writes, Maillart recognizes her change in perspective vis-à-vis the journey, and pinpoints the moment on a visit to Begram, north of Kabul, when she no longer feels driven to continue farther along the road:

> Nowhere else have I listened with more intensity to the rush of a great wind coming down from great mountains. Was it perhaps because I had at last outgrown my need of seeing 'the land beyond the horizon'? Lhassa or Papeete could have loomed ahead, I think, without my heart missing a beat. I had ceased to be proud of having, by my own efforts, turned the world into a playground. (190)

This transition from traveling for travel's sake to the inner journey characterizes the rest of Maillart's entire life. From Kabul, she heads to central and then southern India, where she will live for the duration of the war. She then returns to Switzerland and will spend the next fifty years between her native Geneva and the Alpine village of Chandolin, whose isolated beauty lends itself well to the continued contemplation of the inner journey.

This move toward self-discovery and the inner journey mirrors a shift in travel writing as a whole. Paul Fussel argues in *Abroad: British Traveling Between the Wars* that the onslaught of modern tourism and jet travel following the Second World War signal the end of travel literature, an argument that is not entirely without merit. While travel literature remains alive and well in the twenty-first century, the end of the World War II did signal a change in perspective. Traveling, no longer for the rich and privileged few, becomes for many a commodity like any other.[17] As Eric Leed explains in *The Mind of the Modern Traveler*: "Travel, once an exceptional experience…is now a routine event, as unexceptional as getting into one's car and driving down the road beyond one's usual stopping places…Travel is no longer heroic and individualizing" (287). Leed goes on to note that modernization and globalization effectively mark the end of an era, "a time of sorrow for those who have defined their identities in terms of opposing worlds of others" (288). Leed's description lends itself quite accurately to the situation in which Maillart and Schwarzenbach find themselves at the end of their journey. Perhaps less a time of sorrow than a time of transition, the post-war and post-colonial period of travel writing moves away from the radical Other in favor of the vanishing self. Travel narratives like *The Cruel Way* move toward introspection and autobiography, an indication of the changing nature of the genre.

Notes

1   As explained in chapter two, Ella Maillart wrote *The Cruel Way* in English while living in southern India. Ever critical of her own writing, especially in English, Maillart commented that she found the title *The Cruel Way* far too dramatic when I spoke with her during the summer of 1996.

2   For distances traveled during the trip, see the appendix of the 24 heures edition of *La voie cruelle*.

3   *Die Reise nach Afghanistan 1939–1940* is quoted and referenced here in the French translation, *Où est la terre des promesses? Avec Ella Maillart en Afghanistan 1939–1940*.

4   See Charles Linsmayer's biographical afterward to *Das Glückliche Tal* or *La Vallée heureuse* for a detailed discussion of Schwarzenbach's life. Likewise, see Dominique Miermont's 2004 biography *Annemarie Schwarzenbach ou le mal d'Europe*.

5   The essay "La Steppe" originally appeared in German in the *National-Zeitung* in November 1939. The article was later included in the collection *Où est la terre des promesses? Avec Ella Maillart en Afghanistan (1939–1940)*.

6   For a detailed discussion of the influence of Schwarzenbach's mother in her daughter's life, see Dominique Miermont's *Annemarie Schwarzenbach ou le mal d'Europe*. In 1939, the Schwarzenbach family's Nazi sympathies only strained the mother-daughter relationship even further.

7   Chapter two of Sidonie Smith's *Moving Lives*, entitled "On Foot: Gender at Ground Level," discusses women travelers Isabella Eberhard, Alexandra David-Néel, and Robyn Davidson.

8   Schwarzenbach's *Das glückliche Tal* chronicles, in part, her failed love affair with a young Iranian woman. Likewise, her relationship with American author Carson McCullers ends dismally.

9   Maillart's unpublished letters to Lewis Thompson, part of the Lewis Thompson manuscript collection at Washington State University, and her book *Ti-Puss* elaborate on her understanding of self and the teachings of Hindu philosophy.

10   Maillart traveled through Iran and parts of Afghanistan via bus in 1937.

11   See chapters three and four for discussions of Maillart's treks by foot, horseback, truck, and camel.

12   See Gilles Deleuze and Felix Guattari's *Nomadology: the War Machine*.

13   See Rosi Braidotti's *Nomadic Subjects: Embodiment and Sexual Difference in Contemporary Feminist Theory*.

14   Ria Hackin, French archeologist and friend of Ella Maillart, is at work on a dig in Afghanistan with husband and colleague Joseph Hackin.

15   Schwarzenbach travels north to Kunduz to join Ria and Joseph Hackin at their dig. The arrival of winter weather cuts their work short.

16   As Maillart notes in the final charter of *The Cruel Way*, Schwarzenbach travels
        to the Belgian Congo in 1942 as a war correspondent but is unable to reach the
        French Free Forces there where she had been appointed a journalist. (205). She
        returns to Switzerland later that same year. In the epilogue, Maillart explains
        that Schwarzenbach died as a result of injuries sustained in a bicycle accident
        in November 1942.

17   Clearly, nomadic travel still exists in various forms and as such does not
        qualify as a commodity. The nomadic people of whom Maillart speaks have
        had to alter their traditional lifestyles to accommodate national borders. The
        Roma people, for example, travel throughout Europe as they have done for
        centuries.

Chapter Six

On Travel and Coming Home

Jacques Lacarrière, in his short essay "Le Bernard-l'hermite ou le treizième voyage," makes quick work of categorizing travel and the travel narrative. He promptly distinguishes between those who travel for less noble motivations and true travel writers. As such, he distances himself from business travel, travel for love, exile, deportation, war, tourism, and even adventure.[1] While somewhat tongue in cheek, Lacarriere's essay nonetheless helps define the *Pour une littérature de voyage* movement[2] and helps delimit the context in which we may read Maillart. Lacarrière goes on to discuss the only type of travel of any worth, that which he calls the thirteenth voyage. His definition will help us better come to terms with Ella Maillart's later works and her oeuvre as a whole. According to Lacarrière, the thirteenth voyage can be explained as follows:

> En quoi consiste-t-il ? Il se situe exactement à l'opposé du voyage-éclair. Mais comme il n'existe pas en français un terme unique pour désigner un "déplacement de longue durée de caractère non orageux" je le nommerai : voyage au ralenti, flânerie, musardise. Il consiste à visiter le plus lentement possible êtres et choses, à fréquenter patiemment leur histoire, s'immiscer posément dans leur vie intime. (106)

> [What is it all about ? It is the exact opposite of the quick trip. But no one word exists in French to describe a "lengthy trip, non turbulent in character," so I will call it: a voyage in slow motion, a stroll, a saunter. It involves visiting people and things as slowly as possible, patiently frequenting their history, calmly interfering in their private lives.]

He goes on to comment on the ultimate goals of such a journey: "Le but alors d'un tel voyage ? (. . .) Se vider, se dénuder et une fois vide et nu s'emplir de saveurs et de savoirs nouveaux. Se sentir proche des Lointains et consanguins des Différents" (106). [The goal of such a voyage?...To empty oneself, to strip off one's clothes, and once empty and naked, to fill oneself with new tastes and knowledge. To feel close to those who are Far from you and be closely related to those who are Different.] Lacarrière's comments lend themselves especially well to Maillart's five year stay in Tiruvannamalai, India where she followed the teachings of the Ramana Maharishi, traveled third class, and immersed herself in Indian life. She began to feel that she had more in common with the Indians who spoke Tamil than with English civil servants who frowned upon her living arrangements. Most of all, her time spent in India helps Maillart to articulate her own inner journey, one that brings her to a more clear and long sought after definition of self and the world around her.

While in India, Maillart writes four more travel narratives, including *The Cruel Way*, discussed in chapter five. The other three narratives will be dealt with briefly here in the concluding chapter. These three books fall outside the criteria laid out in the introduction since they either do not focus on travel in the 1930s or do not chronicle a specific journey. The three texts do, however, offer glimpses at the life Maillart led in India and her continued quest for understanding. *Gypsy Afloat* (1942), which Maillart wrote in 1940 shortly after her arrival in India from Afghanistan, marks her shift to writing in English rather than French. Living in southern India, speaking English and bits of Tamil, Maillart decided to write in the lingua franca of her immediate literary environment. *Cruises and Caravans* (1942), written upon request from the American publisher Dent, followed in 1941 and offers a condensed version of the texts Maillart had already published previously as well as short chapters on her childhood, Afghanistan, and India. As such, *Cruises and Caravans* may be read as Maillart's foray into autobiography. Maillart wrote *The Cruel Way* in the fall of 1943, but the book did not appear in print until after the conclusion of the war. Finally, she wrote *Ti-Puss* (1951), her tale of India in the company of her cat—who lends her name to the title—in 1944, shortly before traveling to Tibet and then returning home to Switzerland.

Maillart's return from India to Switzerland marks a significant shift in her lifestyle as she moves away from her previously established pattern of the voyage as such followed by the subsequent manuscript.[3] Indeed, Maillart spends the next fifty years giving talks and lectures, leading groups to India and Nepal, living between Geneva and Chandolin. In Chandolin she finds the atmosphere of peace that she sought in India, and Maillart will spend nearly six months of each year in her alpine retreat. Rather than presenting a biographical or chronological discussion of the fifty years subsequent to Maillart's return from India, this analysis will again refer to literary texts, both by and about Maillart. As such, we will look at some of the letters in the posthumous collection "*Cette Réalité que j'ai pourchassée*" (2003) as well as Anne Deriaz's elegy to Ella Maillart, entitled *Chère Ella* (1998), before considering excerpts from my own interview with Maillart in the summer of 1996. Examining these later texts will provide evidence to show Maillart's notion of home and even travel shifts in these later years as she enters the final stages of the inner journey. In conclusion, this chapter will reconsider Maillart's oeuvre as a whole in the context of twentieth-century travel literature, and more specifically, in travel literature by women.

Gypsy Afloat, the first of the narratives completed in India, chronicles Maillart's time spent on the barge the *Volunteer* in 1925 and 1926. Drawn to the sea after having spent her youth on Lake Geneva, Maillart looks to navigation as an escape from what seems to be otherwise inevitable: working in an office in Switzerland or continuing on as a French teacher in an English boarding school. The book narrates, for the most part, a host of rather technical sailing terms and maneuvers as well as Maillart's tenacious work as first mate. It also, however, offers glimpses of Maillart's life and thoughts while in India, hints that she is moving forward in her pursuit of the inner one. Consider, for example, the opening lines of the preface: "The following pages are nothing more than a few memories of my fickle youth which took place during a fickle moment of the world's life. I have assembled them in an endeavour to sum up my past, outrun it and forget it, once it has helped me to find out what I am" (xi). In her search for self, *Gypsy Afloat* does mark a turning point for Maillart because it represents the end of a dream. In between tales of her stints on the *Volunteer*, Maillart narrates briefly the story of her lifelong friendship with Miette de Saussure, her childhood companion and captain of their mutual sailing expeditions. The two plan to cross the Atlantic with a small crew, following the example of their friend and mentor, French sailor Alain Gerbault.[4] They buy and prepare the sailing ship *Atalante*, preparing for their trans-Atlantic expedition with a two-week fishing trip in the Gulf of Gascogne. Despite Miette's ill health at the time, they cast off for their Atlantic crossing with a crew of four and hopes of eventually heading on to the South Pacific. Much to their mutual disappointment, they must turn back after a short week, Miette too ill to continue. So end their nautical dreams of fleeing Europe for the unspoiled paradise of the islands of the South Pacific. Miette will spend the next six months convalescing while Maillart turns eastward, traveling to Berlin. Much to Maillart's consternation, Miette decides to marry, and the dream of Asia replaces that of navigating the high seas, as Maillart writes: "Once I had broken away from my single-minded hope of making a life at sea, I discovered how strongly the world—Asia particularly—beckoned me" (*Gypsy Afloat* 237). Maillart effectively replaces the sea with the world before her: the end of one adventure thus signals the start of another, and Maillart will travel to Germany before moving on to the newly formed Soviet Union. Only in retrospect does she note the importance of the inner journey: "This life of mine, to what purpose had it been lived, free as it was from any tie?. . . Here again I am dealing with myself. I should explain that I am really writing these pages to find out what I thought fifteen years ago. My log-book never mentions a conversation or a thought" (134). In her youth, Maillart sought adventure and an alternative to life in the city. As she gets older, she looks to attribute a purpose to her wandering, trying to define the very nature of herself.

If *Gypsy Afloat* permits Maillart to begin the process of introspection, then *Ti-Puss* along with letters Maillart wrote from India confirm her progress as she moves farther along the road of the inner journey. Not a conventional travelogue, *Ti-Puss* shares the story of Maillart's life and short travels through India in the company of her cat. More specifically, the cat serves to help Maillart think about love, its qualities, and the relationship to one's inner self. Likewise, in the chapter devoted to southern India in *Cruises and Caravans*, Maillart elaborates further on her choice to remain five years in India, explaining briefly the goals she has set for herself, and her continued quest for understanding.

Maillart finds herself in southern India in late 1939, having recently completed the journey from Geneva to Kabul by car. Exhausted by the time and effort devoted to her companion, Annemarie Schwarzenbach, unsure of what to do in the face of the Second World War, Maillart opts to remain in India, convinced that the knowledge of self will lead to the peace that eludes her personally and Europe collectively. As Maillart explains in *Croisières et caravans:*[5] "L'enseignement que donne les livres ne me convenant pas, je voulais vivre longtemps auprès d'un sage dont le comportement pourrait me faire saisir ce que mon manque de préparation intellectuelle me rendait incompréhensible" (299). [Book learning did not suit me, and I wanted to live for a long period of time near a sage whose behavior could help me understand that which my lack of intellectual preparation made incomprehensible to me.] Drawn to the Ramana Maharishi, Maillart thus embarks on a voyage unlike the many others she has undertaken to date: "Here in India I have started on a new journey which, I know, will take me further than before towards the perfect life I was instinctively seeking. I began this journey by exploring the unmapped territory of my own mind" (*Cruises and Caravans* 154).The metaphorical voyage takes place at the same time that Maillart travels sporadically throughout southern and central India, sometimes in search of a respite from the heat, sometimes simply to visit friends. As Lacarrière suggests in the essay cited earlier, Maillart comes to feel close to those who differ from her most. Although a white European, she lives and travels modestly. As she explains in *Ti-Puss*:

> For the last two years I had traveled cheaply—not only for economy's sake, but also in order to observe that seething humanity surrounding me, since I had few opportunities to be with the people. Though we could not speak, my neighbors were friendly. In the higher classes I was studied suspiciously by white women who could not place me—wives of missionaries, of Anglo-Indian railway officials, of cotton-firms' managers, of civil servants. (27)

Maillart thus identifies with her Indian neighbors more readily than with English colonials. Interestingly enough, this identification is neither linguistic nor religious, but apparently one based primarily on class. While Maillart does not fit into the caste system rigidly adhered to by her neighbors in the train or in her neighborhood, she works to understand their behavior and to create a sort of solidarity between herself and those around her. She refuses to adhere to the stereotypes

associated with white, European women. As such, Maillart opts for
the sort of travel advocated by Lacarrière.

Her perpetual lack of funds aligns her with those who travel third
class and distances her from some of her compatriots. In a letter to her
mother dated 1940, Maillart is quick to note that her financial circumstances separate her from, for example, her former traveling companion, Annemarie Schwarzenbach:

> Je ne suis pas en mesure de dépenser, comme Annemarie, "à fonds
> perdus", et de simplement jeter un coup d'œil sur ces pays lointains.
> Qui plus est, ce sera probablement le dernier grand voyage que je
> pourrai jamais entreprendre ; j'essayerai donc de le rendre aussi
> intéressant que possible. (*Cette Réalité que j'ai pourchassée* 142)

> [I am not in a position, like Annemarie, to spend as much as I like and
> simply to take a quick look at these far-away countries. In addition, this
> will probably be the last major voyage that I will ever be able to
> undertake; hence, I will try to make it as interesting as possible.]

India will represent, in fact, the last period of extended travel for
Maillart, just as she suggests in her letter. During her time spent there,
she lives quietly near the sage, accompanied by her cat Ti-Puss in
many of her daily activities. In her eyes, the cat symbolizes the perfection that Maillart seeks to understand (*Ti-Puss* 68).

Her search for perfection and peace will not last for ever. Maillart
realizes that at some point she will be obliged to return to the Occident. As such, she seeks to put her time to the best use, and wonders
to what end she continues to write travel narratives. In another letter
to her mother in 1941, Maillart questions the way in which she has, to
date, earned her living:

> D'autre part tu sais que je ne suis pas écrivain dans l'âme ; et avant de
> continuer à écrire des livres imparfaits autant qu'inutiles, cela faut la
> peine de réfléchir. L'endroit ici n'est pas mal choisi pour cette activité ;
> et puis voilà j'ai 38 ans, une vingtaine d'années derrière moi—et peut-
> être autant devant moi pour trouver cette Réalité que j'ai pourchassée
> jusqu'ici sur terre et sur mer . (*Cette Réalité que j'ai pourchassée* 152)

> [On the other hand, you know that I am not a writer at heart. Before
> continuing to write books that are as flawed as they are useless, it is
> worth taking some time to think. This is not a bad place for such activ-
> ity. Here I am at thirty-eight, twenty or so years behind me and perhaps

as many ahead of me, to find this Reality that I have pursued thus far, both on land and on sea.]

At this point, Maillart confirms that her time in India will serve as a spiritual guide for her future, noting that

Il n'est pas dit que je sache la trouver cette Réalité que les sages affirment être en chacun. Mais tout au moins je peux essayer. Je ne pars pas pour savoir le comment, pourquoi et quand de tout, mais afin d'établir en moi une boussole de bonne qualité afin de ne plus perdre la tête à tout moment. (152)

[There is no guarantee that I will find this Reality that the sages affirm exists within each of us. But at least I can try. I am not leaving to know the how, why, and when of everything, but rather to establish within me a reliable compass so that I won't lose my head at the slightest provocation.]

Maillart strives to explain further this ongoing search for self in *Croisières et caravans*:

Armés de patience, il nous faut au contraire continuer à vivre normalement, mais en cherchant quelle est la nature de ce "je" qui surgit à chaque instant lorsqu'on dit : je pense, j'agis, je ressens, je suis… Cette enquête ne peut pas être qualifiée de démarche égoïste car elle contribue à détruire notre *ego*—cette fausse entité qui nous divise et nous sépare de notre être vrai ; on peut tenter de définir ce dernier par les mots : amour et lumière consciente, illimitée.
En démasquant constamment cette fausse entité, nous parviendrons à nous fixer dans l'être vrai : l'irréductible division de notre monde entre sujet et objet, disparaîtra. (306–7)

[Armed with patience, we should continue to live normally, while searching for the nature of the "I" that arises each time we say: I think, I act, I feel, I am…This inquiry cannot be considered selfish because it contributes to the destruction of our *ego*—this false entity that divides us and separates us from our true being; we can try to define the latter with words: love and conscious light, unlimited.
By constantly unmasking this false entity, we will succeed in securing ourselves in the true being: our world's irreducible division between subject and object will then disappear.]

This continued quest for the true being, the one that moves beyond the subject/object dichotomy, marks the rest of Maillart's long life.

At the war's end, Maillart leaves India and returns to Switzerland. She spends the summer of 1946 in painter Edmond Bille's[6] chalet in Chandolin at his suggestion: "Edmond Bille m'a dit : 'Qu'est-ce que vous avez mauvaise mine, Ella ! Je vais vous prêter mon chalet de Chandolin, à 2000 mètres et en trois mois vous allez vous refaire une santé.' C'est exactement ce qui s'est produit" (Deriaz 104). ["Edmond Bille said to me: 'You are so pale, Ella! I am going to lend you my chalet in Chandolin, at 2000 meters, and in three months, you will be back to your old self.'" "That's exactly what happened."] Enamored with the beauty of the Alpine retreat, Maillart has her own chalet, *Atchala*, built in Chandolin two years later. The construction of the chalet undoubtedly indicates that Maillart, for the first time, abandons, in a sense, her travels in order to set down roots. In fact, Chandolin becomes a home for her akin only perhaps to Maillart's childhood retreat on Lake Geneva. This shift from constant travel to a more sedentary existence, from wandering nomad to settled citizen, is also reflected in her life's pursuits. Travel is no longer an end in itself but rather a means toward further reflection on the inner journey.

Maillart lived alone, alternating between the family apartment in Geneva and the chalet in Chandolin, until she was over ninety years old. At the age of ninety-two, she gained a companion and a confidant. Anne Deriaz, writer and teacher from Geneva, helped Maillart with the details of daily life when Maillart was no longer able to do entirely for herself. Their relationship is described in Anne Deriaz's *Chère Ella*, and her narrative offers a unique look at yet another stage of the inner journey. As Anne Deriaz writes to Maillart in the letter that serves as a prologue to her book:

> Vous aviez longtemps marché sur la Terre, sans moi.
> Et lorsque votre pas se fut ralenti, que votre marche devint difficile, je vous ai massé les pieds. Et vous m'avez demandé de vous accompagner.
> Alors a commencé pour nous deux une sorte de voyage.
> Dans le temps ordinaire et l'espace quotidien. (22)

> [You walked for a long time on this Earth without me.
> And when your step slowed, when walking became difficult, I massaged your feet. And you asked me to accompany you.
> So began a sort of journey for the two of us.
> In ordinary time and everyday spaces.]

These steps in ordinary time and space will come to confirm the transformation away from the life of constant displacement. Indeed, if the construction of her chalet *Atchala* signals the setting of new roots, her final years in Chandolin confirm that the roots have taken hold, as Anne Deriaz eloquently explains: "Je vous écoutais./ J'observais./ L'enracinement de votre corps superbe dans la terre de ce lieu" (34). [I listened to you./I observed./Your splendid body entrenched in the earth, in this place.] If Ella Maillart's prose and early correspondence indicate an itinerant notion of home, one that has no specific boundaries and is inexorably linked to the love of travel,[7] the end of her life and Deriaz's narrative point to a rootedness that comes with having made Chandolin her true home. Maillart confirms the attraction that Chandolin holds for her in a quote later recorded by Deriaz: "Je ne pouvais plus quitter cet endroit. Tu me comprends puisque tu as vécu presque la même chose./ Je rentrais des Indes. Je voulais revenir en Europe. A Chandolin, je me sentais près de Dieu. Ici, tu vois, c'est un endroit unique au monde" (105). ["I couldn't leave this place. You understand me since you experienced nearly the same thing. I had just returned from India. I wanted to come back to Europe. In Chandolin, I felt close to God. Here, you see, is a unique place in the world."] Indeed, Maillart literally reigns over much of the village, like a queen over her court, occasionally deigning to speak to her followers, at other times guarding her silence, as Deriaz describes: "Vous étiez assise à une longue table, entourée d'amis. C'était, je crois, pour la plupart des femmes. Elles vous parlaient. Vous ne répondiez pas. Ces femmes auraient pu être une cour, votre cour" (25). [You were seated at a long table, surrounded by friends. They were, I believe, for the most part, women. They were speaking to you. You didn't answer. These women could have been your court and you their queen.] Sovereign ruler of her Alpine retreat, Maillart created *Atchala* in the image of her wanderings, thus reuniting her past and present. Her chalet echoes her travels and experience, everything fastidiously placed and ordered, a precision that recalls her year as a sailor and the need to use small places well. She lives surrounded by her books and reminders of her voyages. As Anne Deriaz explains: "Dans votre bureau chaque objet avait une histoire. Echo de votre propre histoire. Jalon dans votre quête" (78). [In your study, each object had a history. An echo of your own history. A marker in your quest.] As the chalet and its possessions remind Maillart and the reader of the kilometers traveled, of the people and places encountered along the way, Chandolin and its beauty encourage progress of the inner journey. Chandolin seems to reunite divergent aspects of Maillart's past:

> Pourquoi Chandolin ?
> A cause de la richesse de l'eau peut-être. Qui court partout. Au printemps.
> "L'eau. L'eau, c'est la liberté. Tu es sur l'eau et personne ne peut t'empêcher. Tu es libre.
> "Tu comprends, quand tu es en mer, seule, que tu dois veiller, prendre garde aux cargos qui risquent de t'avaler, tu te dis : Dieu existe.
> "Quand je naviguais seule, proche de l'eau et de l'air, je ressentais Dieu. Et quand je montais en montagne, je m'approchais de Dieu". (Deriaz 47)

> [Why Chandolin?
> Perhaps because of the wealth of water. Which flows everywhere. In the spring.
> "Water. Water is freedom. You are out on the water and no one can stop you. You are free.
> "You understand, when you are alone at sea, that you have to be vigilant, be careful of the cargo ships that might swallow you up, you say to yourself: God exists.
> When I sailed alone, so close to the water and the air, I could feel God. And when I went up to the mountain, I moved closer to God."]

This synthesis of water and mountain, fresh air and spectacular views, lends itself quite naturally to meditation. Chandolin seems to provide the necessary space for Maillart to bring closure to her journey toward the essential oneness that she seeks. As Anne Deriaz observes, quoting her mentor: "Regarde ce paysage grandiose. Il incite à la méditation. Il m'empêche de me disperser. Cette beauté, la densité du silence m'aident et me ramènent sans cesse à l'essentiel. J'écoute Dieu me parler dans ce silence" (53). ["Look at this magnificent landscape. It invites meditation. It stops me from losing myself. This beauty, the density of the silence, helps me and constantly brings me back to the essential. I listen to God speak to me in this silence."] In Deriaz's narrative, Maillart's voice intertwines with the author's, their dialogue progressing much like a voyage in itself. Deriaz returns to this metaphor periodically throughout the text, effectively melding past and present. As such, a simple turn on the balcony launches a journey anew at a time when Maillart can no longer move easily on her own:

"Vers l'ouest, c'est tellement humain. Au sud, on se sent grandiose! Comme le paysage!...J'ai fait un quart de tour et j'ai l'impression d'avoir voyagé!"

C'était le voyage à la recherche de l'Unité. Et ce voyage se faisait dans le silence et l'immobilité. (83)

["To the west, it's so human. To the south, we feel so magnificent! Like the landscape!...And this magnificent landscape invites us to meditate. I turn around and I have the impression that I have traveled!"

That was the voyage in search of Unity. And this voyage took place in silence and immobility.]

Maillart's final years are thus traced in the story of this double voyage, one that carries forward Ella Maillart and Anne Deriaz. As Deriaz suggests above, this journey completed in silence and immobility would be slow and sometimes arduous, perhaps the most challenging voyage of Maillart's long life. Deriaz neither takes this task lightly, nor does she enter into the situation unaware: "J'avais la ferme conviction que Dieu me demandait précisément de vous accompagner pendant cette dernière étape de votre voyage terrestre. Car c'était un voyage que nous faisions ensemble. Avec des étapes. Presque deux ans" (95). [I had the firm conviction that God was asking me specifically to accompany you during this final stage of your earthly journey. Because it was a journey that we embarked upon together. With different stages. Nearly two years.] Deriaz's account of these two years offers a satisfying conclusion to a lifelong quest, implying that Maillart not only arrived at the essential oneness that she sought, but that the mentor also came to appreciate the camaraderie offered by her caregiver and disciple of sorts. Anne Deriaz, for her part, recognizes the subtle signals that indicate the end of a journey that lasted more than ninety years: "Je le sentais bien, c'était l'étape finale de votre double voyage : l'un extérieur, à la recherche d'un paradis sur terre, et l'autre intérieur, à la recherche de l'Immuable que vous appeliez souvent Dieu" (125). [I could feel it, this was the final stage of your dual journey: the one exterior, in search of heaven on earth, and the other interior, in search of the Eternal, what you often called God.]

I had the opportunity to speak with both Ella Maillart and Anne Deriaz in June 1996, the beginning of Maillart's final summer in her beloved Chandolin. Already at that point, Deriaz spent much of her time with Maillart, and warned me that she did not quite understand why the older Maillart was willing to have me come speak to her. I explained that Maillart and I had visited once the year before in her apartment in Geneva and had corresponded intermittently. We agreed that Maillart was pleased to have an American academic show real interest in her work. Speaking with Anne Deriaz and Ella Maillart as I admired the view from *Atchala* confirmed for me what *Chère Ella* clearly shows: Maillart's sense of having put down roots along with her love of Chandolin transformed her notion of home. Likewise, travel took on another meaning during the final years of her life. Chandolin thus became Maillart's final resting point, the arrival point for the inner journey.

At the time of my interview with Maillart, I was just beginning my research, and in retrospect, had not prepared particularly useful questions for her. Furthermore, I realized when I sat down with Maillart, that despite her age, she was far more savvy than the naïve assistant professor from Oregon. As such, Ella did most of the interviewing, finding out more about me than I learned about her. One gathers as much from the opening remarks as I begin taping our interview, fumbling with the tape recorder: "EM: Vous savez vous en servir? / SSB: Plus ou moins, oui. / EM: Vous avez l'air débutante" . (Personal interview, 11 June 1996). [EM: Do you know how to use that? / SSB: Yes, more or less. /EM: You look like a real beginner.][8] Novice indeed, I did my best with the two hours that followed. The excerpts I include here are purely anecdotal, but serve to show that Maillart's past informed her present until the end of her life. Consider this brief discussion on women writers and writing in English:

> EM: Il y a beaucoup d'Anglaises qui ont écrit.
> SSB: Oui.
> EM: Elles ont vraiment la palme, elles ont écrit de bons livres. En principe, Freya Starke était la meilleure comme écrivain de voyages.[9] Mon anglais c'était au pis-aller. Je n'ai jamais…J'avais un très bon ami aux Indes qui essayait de corriger mes livres en anglais. Il m'a dit, Lewis Thompson, m'a dit : "Je ne comprends pas que vous avez l'audace ou que tu as l'audace d'écrire en anglais alors que tu n'as jamais bien appris l'anglais. C'est un mépris de cette langue." C'était un poète je dois dire. Et alors, c'est bien vrai que ne sachant pas très bien le français parce que je lisais tout le temps des livres d'aventure anglais—mon français était nul—je me suis rabattue sur l'anglais en disant au moins avec l'anglais, on ne peut pas m'accuser, ce n'est pas ma langue. J'avais donc une excuse. On ne peut pas, oui, me dire que j'écris mal. Alors, ça vous pouvez le répéter parfaitement, je savais que je ne savais pas l'anglais. Et c'était pratique parce qu'il y avait partout des dictionnaires

anglais [en Inde]. Parce qu'au fond, j'ai toujours aimé les gros écrivains français et je savais que mon français n'était pas bon. Mes parents étaient...j'avais une mère danoise et un papa suisse allemand, et mon français à l'école était très quelconque, donc je n'avais pas de prétentions d'être bon écrivain en français. Enfin, l'anglais était au pis-aller pour ne pas mourir de faim. Non, je vous dis tout cela parce qu'on me demande parfois pourquoi je n'ai pas écrit dans ma langue. (Personal interview, 11 June 1996).

[EM: Many English women have written.
SSB: Yes.
EM: They wear the crown, they wrote some very fine books. In principle, Freya Starke was the best of the travel writers. My English was a last resort. I had never...I had a very good friend in India who tried to correct my books in English. He, Lewis Thompson that is, told me: "I don't understand how you can have the audacity to write in English when you never learned English well. What contempt for this language." I should add that he was a poet. At the time, it is perfectly true that not knowing French very well because I had read adventure books in English constantly—my French was terrible—and decided to make do with English, saying to myself that at least with English, no one could blame me since it was not my language. So, I had an excuse. That way no one could tell me that I write badly. You can certainly repeat that to anyone who asks: I knew that I did not know English. But it was practical because there were English dictionaries everywhere [in India]. Basically, I had always liked the great French writers and I knew that my French was not good. My parents were...my mother was Danish and my father Swiss-German, and my French at school was very average, so I had no illusions of being a good writer in French. Finally, English was a last resort so I wouldn't starve. No, I am just telling you all this because people sometimes ask me why I didn't write in my language.]

Modesty aside, having written in both French and English makes Maillart's travel narratives even more difficult to categorize. As noted in the introductory chapter, because she was neither English nor French, but wrote in both English and French, critics have trouble locating Ella Maillart on the map of the twentieth-century travel narrative.

Maillart did, however, as she reminded me in our interview, travel great distances with some of the most famous travelers of the time, including Peter Fleming and Annemarie Schwarzenbach. She spoke of Fleming with me at some length:

EM: Bon, il [Fleming] était intelligent, mais il savait que j'avais écrit *Turkestan Solo*, et il avait un petit peu de respect pour moi. Mais, il était très lié avec la meilleure actrice de Londres, une femme de très grande beauté, Celia Johnson. Il était un homme arrivé, dont les livres se vendait très bien. Alors moi, j'ai un peu pris, enfin c'était plus fort que moi, la technique de, pas de tourner en boule, c'est trop fort ce que je dis, mais de pouvoir blaguer avec lui. Mais c'était un très bon moyen de correspondance qui a très bien marché. Moi, je savais qu'il avait une liaison avec une des femmes les plus célèbres de Londres, et puis moi, ce n'était pas mon type. Il était très, très lettré, et moi, je n'avais jamais eu de prétentions pour devenir une femme de lettres. Enfin, on s'est très bien entendu, si vous avez lu le livre, ce n'est pas la peine de vous en parler.

SSB : Oui, mais il me semble que vous aviez tous les deux des caractères assez forts.

EM : Mais, je crois qu'entre gens intelligents on peut s'entendre. On se prend pas au sérieux. Il n'y a pas de drame, enfin, c'est mon expérience. Mais alors, j'avais donc voyagé avec des caravanes dans le Turkestan russe, donc je savais peut-être un tout petit peu plus de lui au point de vue de chameaux. Ça m'a rendu service.

SSB : C'était différent, je pense, de voyager avec Annemarie Schwarzenbach dans le Ford à travers l'Afghanistan.

EM : Mais naturellement, moi, j'ai toujours mieux aimé les hommes que les femmes. Les femmes, je les trouvais bêtes : elles avaient peur, elles ne connaissaient rien, elles n'avaient pas lu. Ô, il y a des femmes intelligentes, naturellement, mais par instinct, j'étais sportive en ski, en bateau à voile, il y avait peu de femmes avec qui je m'entendais. Mais, je suis arrivée à faire ce que je voulais. (Personal interview, 11 June 1996)

[EM: Well, he [Fleming] was intelligent and he knew I had written *Turkestan Solo* and had a little bit of respect for me. But he was in a relationship with the best actress in London, a woman of great beauty, Celia Johnson. He was already quite successful, so his books sold very well. As for me, I got into the habit, I couldn't really help myself, of making fun of him, no, that is perhaps too strong, but of joking with him. This manner of communication worked out well for us. As for me, I knew quite well that he had a relationship with one of the most famous women in London, and he was not my type. He was very, very well-read and as for me, I had never any illusions of becoming a woman of letters. In the end, we got along very well, and if you read the book, it is not worth talking about.

SSB: Yes, but it seems to me that you both had rather strong characters.

EM: But I think that intelligent people can get along. We don't take ourselves too seriously. In my experience, there is no drama there. But then, I had already traveled with caravans in Russian Turkistan, so I knew perhaps a little bit more than him as far as camels were concerned. That helped me considerably.

SSB: It must have been quite different, I would think, traveling with Annemarie Schwarzenbach in the Ford across Afghanistan.

EM: It goes without saying that I always liked men more than women. I found women silly: they were afraid, they didn't know anything, they hadn't read. Oh, there are intelligent women, of course, but by instinct—I was athletic, involved in skiing and sailing—there were few women with whom I got along well. But, I was able to do as I wanted.]

Understandably hesitant to speak about the tragic life and death of her former traveling companion, Maillart's words, nonetheless, sum up a life well lived. She, indeed, was able to do what she wanted.

Having lived her life fully and freely, Maillart traced the path of one of the great travelers and travel writers of the twentieth-century. As Laurence Deonna notes in the section of *Les Femmes dans la mémoire de Genève* (2005) devoted to travel and "les grandes voyageuses," Maillart belongs to a small group of elite travelers in the French-speaking world, several of whom were Swiss. Indeed, in the June 2004 *Magazine littéraire*, of the fifteen or so travel writers of note, five hail from Switzerland and three are women (Deonna 278). As Deonna explains: "Mais la vraie surprise est ailleurs: les trois autres Suisses nommés au Top Ten des bourlingueurs d'hier (…) sont des bourlinguères ! Comme quoi le droit de vote n'est pas un *must* lorsqu'une femme s'est mis dans sa tête de pioche de courir le monde" (278). [But the real surprise is elsewhere: the three other Swiss named to the Top Ten wanderers of yesterday (…) are women! Which just goes to show you that the right to vote is not a *must* when a woman has gotten it into her hard head to travel the world.] Membership in the exclusive club of famous travelers offers no guarantees, however. As Brigitte Mantilleri explains in the brief article devoted to Maillart in *Les Femmes dans la mémoire de Genève* :

> Pourtant, rien ne nous assure qu'elle [Maillart] aura l'honneur suprême de survivre à son époque, de rester dans la mémoire collective, d'être citée en exemple aux générations suivantes. Car bien que ses œuvres soient répertoriées, ses photographies (environ 16'000 clichés) léguées au Musée de l'Elysée à Lausanne et qu'une fondation ait été créée en son nom, elle a un handicap majeur, Ella. Elle est femme et les femmes, jusqu'à présent, n'ont pas marqué l'Histoire, qu'elle soit politique, littéraire, artistique ou autre. Pourquoi ? Parce qu'elles glissent habituellement entre les mailles du filet de la mémoire : oubliées dans

les encyclopédies, omises dans les livres d'histoire, clairsemées dans les volumes de la Pléaide, ignorées dans les volumes qui répertorient les "Grands Hommes" de Genève ou ailleurs. (281)

[However, nothing assures us that she [Maillart] will have the supreme honor of outliving her own era, of remaining in the collective memory, of being cited as an example to future generations. Because even if her works have been indexed, her photographs (approximately 16,000 negatives) bequeathed to the Museé de l'Elysée in Lausanne, and a foundation created in her name, Ella still has a major handicap. She is a woman and women, until the present day, have not marked History, whether it be political, literary, artistic or otherwise. Why? Because they typically slip through the net of memory: forgotten in encyclopedias, left out of history books, few and far between in the volumes of the Pléaide, ignored in the volumes that index the "Great Men" of Geneva or elsewhere.]

This notion of finding one's place in history/ History brings us back to several of the conundrums presented in the opening chapter: how should we classify Maillart so as to assure her oeuvre a space in literary history? Mantilleri's short analysis may not offer any particularly novel observations, but at the same time, she reminds us of what we know to be all too true: women writers and travelers, especially women outside the Hexagon, slip from the collective memory with surprising alacrity. With this in mind, it is worth revisiting how we consider Ella Maillart and her work within the greater body of travel literature.

Charles Forsdick broaches this subject in his article "Hidden journeys: gender, genre and twentieth-century travel literature in French." One of the few critics to consider Maillart in his analysis, Forsdick mentions her work in the context of the *Pour une littérature de voyage* movement cited at the beginning of this chapter. He points to the very subjective nature of the choice of travel writers included in the *Pour une littérature de voyage* movement, noting the exclusion of women authors, with the exception of Ella Maillart:

This inevitably selective, subjective catalogue...conflates, as is perhaps appropriate for the intergeneric, transgeneric glory-hole represented by the 'genre d'accueil' known as travel literature, a diverse selection of material (contemporary works and re-editions; French-language texts and translations; travel accounts, essays and biographies). Again the genre is heavily gendered: three texts by Ella Maillart, all dating from the 1930s and 1940s (and 'rediscovered', shortly before their author's death, in the 1990s), are smuggled in, but Maillart is granted an ambiguous status somewhere between *doyenne* of the present movement and anachronistic remnant of a tradition of eccentric Victorian lady travelers.[10] (316)

Forsdick goes on to use the "anachronistic remnant of a tradition of eccentric Victorian lady travelers" as a springboard for his brief discussion of women's travel writing contemporary to the *Pour une littérature de voyage* movement. Forsdick's criticism of the movement for its failure to include women does not resolve itself easily. Forsdick himself seems somewhat hard-pressed to place Maillart's oeuvre centrally in the context of the movement or even in the more vast context of twentieth-century travel writing in general:

While some women travelers might aim to forge an *écriture [de voyage] feminine*, founded in mistrust of the rhetoric of mastery, conquest and colonization, others, such as Ella Maillart, share many discursive characteristics with those of their male contemporaries. A more common practice, however, is a process of sharing (and subsequent appropriation or tailoring) of those practical strategies and literary forms or figures adopted and developed by male writers to trace their own journeys. (317)

While I would not argue with the notion that Ella Maillart shares many discursive characteristics with her male contemporaries, this study has shown how Maillart has adapted practical and discursive strategies to trace her many travels as well as the inner journey. Clearly, Forsdick had no intention of providing a detailed reading of Maillart's work, but his comments leave the reader with the sentiment that Maillart is merely an afterthought, an exceptional addition to a movement centered on male writers. Forsdick concludes by advocating for a contextual approach to travel narratives in the twentieth century, suggesting that the potentially volatile insertion of female texts into the greater body of travel literature should be handled delicately:

Women's travel narratives have a (proto-)feminist agenda of supplying alternative paradigms of women's place in society, opening up alternative perspectives on elsewhere; at the same time, however, they have the potential to disrupt, through comparison, the assumptions...that tie male travelers to their journeys. A separatist view of women's travel writing is to be avoided, for not only does it conflate a variety of journeys (and the subjectivities on which they depend) into a falsely unified

> repository of female experience, but also it risks replicating the divisions which the *Pour une littérature voyageuse* movement tends to perpetuate. (322)

Forsdick's contention that a separatist view of women's travel writing is to be avoided seems to assure exclusion of Maillart and others from our broader discussion of travel literature. For, while I would certainly agree that the conflation of journeys and their corresponding subjectivities might create a "falsely unified repository of female experience," I would argue that relegating women's travel to the fringes of male-dominated movements like *Pour une littérature voyageuse* virtually ensures the loss of women's travel writing into the abyss of History. Instead, I would advocate and have argued here for a discussion of women travelers and their travel narratives in their own right as well as in the context of male-dominated movements, a discussion that is inclusive rather than exclusive, one that embraces a variety of perspectives, subjectivities, and experiences. Only by creating a *Pour une littérature voyageuse* for "les voyageuses" can we assure that they will earn a more permanent place in print and in the collective memory. As Brigitte Mantilleri notes in the conclusion to her recent article: "Mais qui sait? Ella Maillart a dit: 'L'impossible recule devant celui qui avance'. Elle réussira peut-être à faire avancer la cause des héroïnes et à rester dans notre mémoire" (281). [But who knows? Ella Maillart once said: "The impossible retreats in the face of those who move forward." She will perhaps succeed in moving forward the heroines' cause and remain in our memory.] Creating a space for the noteworthy travel writings of Ella Maillart should hardly be considered the impossible. Studies like this one should serve to bring Ella Maillart into the critical center, assuring her presence in the collective memory of women travelers and travel writers.

Notes

1. See Jacques Lacarrière, "Le Bernard-l'hermite ou le treizième voyage" in *Pour une littérature voyageuse* (105).

2. Charles Forsdick explains the *Pour une littérature de voyage* movement as "a loose grouping of authors which emerged in the 1970s and 1980s and was consolidated in 1990 with the *Etonnants Voyageurs* festival in Saint-Malo" (315) in his article "Hidden Journeys: gender, genre and 20th-century travel literature in French."

3. Maillart did write *The Land of the Sherpas*, published by Stodder and Houghton in London in 1955, after traveling in 1951 to Nepal. The book met with little popular or critical success, and was never translated into French like her other narratives originally written in English. The photographs Maillart took during that and subsequent trips to Nepal are included in *La Vie immediate* (1991), a tribute to the collection of photographs and negatives that Maillart left to the Musée de l'Elysée in Lausanne.

4. Gerbault became the first to sail solo across the Atlantic from east to west in 1923.

5. The original English version of *Cruises and Caravans* (1942) cited here does not include the final chapter of the French translation, *Croisières et Caravans* (1950). Hence, the title is quoted in French when referring specifically to the French text. Translations of quotes from the final chapter are my own.

6. Edmond Bille, father of writer Corinna Bille and originally from Neuchatel, moved to Sion and lived and worked in the canton of Valais.

7. For a detailed discussion of Maillart's correspondence and the notion of home, see Margaret McColley's recent dissertation "The Epistolary Self: Home and Identity in Franchophone Women's Travel Letters (1850–1950)."

8. Ella Maillart, interview with the author, June 1996.

9. Freya Starke (1893–1993) traveled all over the Middle East, Greece, Italy, and Turkey. Best known for her travel narrative *The Valley of the Assassins* (1934), Starke corresponded periodically with Ella Maillart throughout their lives.

10. I read Maillart's inclusion in the movement somewhat differently. I suspect that Nicolas Bouvier, for whom Ella Maillart was both a mentor and friend, may have inserted her travelogues among those of the *Pour une littérature de voyage* movement.

Bibliography

Afghanistan Online. Ed. Abdullah Qazi. 2005. 11 March 2005 <http://www.afghan-web.com/history/articles/reshtya.html>.

Aiken, Susan Hardy. "Writing (in) Exile: Isak Dinesen and the Poetics of Displacement." *Women's Writing in Exile*. Chapel Hill: University of North Carolina Press, 1989. Mary Lynn Broe and Angela Ingram, eds. 113–132.

Armel, Aliette. "Ella Maillart, la quête de l'harmonie." *Magazine Littéraire* 432 (2004): 50–1.

———. "Annemarie Schwarzenbach, condamnée à l'exil et à l'aventure." *Magazine Littéraire* 432 (2004): 51–2.

Barthes, Roland. *La Chambre claire : Note sur la photographie*. Paris: Gallimard / Seuil, 1980.

Benstock, Shari. "Expatriate Modernism: Writing on the Cultural Rim." *Women's Writing in Exile*. Chapel Hill: University of North Carolina Press, 1989. Mary Lynn Broe and Angela Ingram, eds. 19–40.

de Biasi, Pierre-Marc. "Flaubert, une conversion du regard." *Magazine Littéraire* 432 (2004): 42–44

Bille, S. Corinna. *La demoiselle sauvage : nouvelles*. 1974. Paris: Gallimard, 1992.

Bonadei, Rossana. "Theory into *écriture*: travel literature encounters touring cultures." *Cross-Cultural Travel: Papers from the Royal Irish Academy International Symposium on Literature and Travel*. Ed. Jane Conroy. Travel Writing Across the Disciplines 7. New York: Peter Lang, 2002. 417–428.

Borer, Alain et al. *Pour une littérature voyageuse*. Brussels: Editions Complexe, 1999.

Bouvier, Nicolas. *Chronique japonaise*. 1975. Paris: Payot, 1989.

———. "La Clé des champs." *Pour une littérature voyageuse*. 1992. Brussels: Editions Complexe, 1999. 41–44.

———. *L'Echappée belle: éloge de quelques pérégrins*. Geneva: Metropolis, 1996.

———. "Petite morale portative." *Pour une littérature voyageuse*. Brussels: Editions Complexe, 1999. 45–56.

———. *Le poisson-scorpion*. 1982. Paris: Folio Gallimard, 1996.

———. *L'usage du monde*. 1963. Paris: Payot, 1992.

Braidotti, Rosi. *Nomadic Subjects: Embodiment and Sexual Difference in Contemporary Feminist Theory*. New York: Columbia UP, 1994.

Chatwin, Bruce. *In Patagonia*. London: Jonathan Cape, 1977.

Clark, Steve. Introduction. *Travel Writing and Empire: Postcolonial Theory in Transit*. Ed. Steve Clark. New York: Zed, 1999. 1–28.

Clifford, James. *Routes: Travel and Translation in the Late Twentieth Century*. Cambridge, MA: Harvard UP, 1997.

Conroy, Jane. Introduction. *Cross-Cultural Travel: Papers from the Royal Irish Academy International Symposium on Literature and Travel.* Ed. Jane Conroy. Travel Writing Across the Disciplines 7. New York: Peter Lang, 2002. xii–xxii.

David-Néel, Alexandra. Letter to Ella Maillart, 23 December 1950. Ella Maillart Collection. Manuscript Collection, Bibliothèque publique et universitaire, Geneva.

———. *Voyage d'une Parisienne à Lhassa.* 1927. Paris: Plon, 1982.

Deleuze, Gilles, and Felix Guattari. *Nomadology: the War Machine.* Trans. Brian Massumi. New York: Columbia UP/Semiotext(e), 1986.

Delon, Michel. "Du côté du Sin-Kiang." Rev. of *Oasis interdites,* by Ella Maillart. *Magazine Littéraire* 272 (1989): 59.

Dibie, Pascal. "Le voyage ethnologique." *Magazine Littéraire* 432 (2004): 56–7.

Donna, Laurence. "Les grandes voyageuses." *Les Femmes dans la mémoire de Genève: Du XVe au XXe siècle.* Eds. Erica Deuber Ziegler and Natalia Tikhonov. Geneva: Editions Suzanne Hurter, 2005. 278–279.

Deriaz, Anne. *Chère Ella: élégie pour Ella Maillart.* Arles: Actes Sud, 1998.

Eberhardt, Isabelle. *Lettres et journalières.* Arles: Actes sud, 1987.

Fabre, Eugène. "Ella au pays des Soviets. Le livre de l'aventureuse. " Rev. of *Parmi la jeunesse russe,* by Ella Maillart. *La Suisse* 1932.

———. "Un livre d'Ella Maillart. " Rev. of *Des Monts célestes aux sables rouges,* by Ella Maillart. *La Suisse* 22 May 1934.

Fleming, Peter. *News from Tartary.* 1936. Evanston, IL: Northwestern University Press, 1999.

Forsdick, Charles. "Hidden journeys: gender, genre and twentieth-century travel literature in French." *Cross-Cultural Travel: Papers from the Royal Irish Academy International Symposium on Literature and Travel.* Ed. Jane Conroy. Travel Writing Across the Disciplines 7. New York: Peter Lang, 2002. 315–323.

———."Sa(l)vaging Exoticism: New Approaches to 1930s Travel Literature in French." *Cultural Encounters : European Travel Writing in the 1930s.* Eds. Charles Burdett and Derek Duncan. New York : Berghahn Books, 2002. 29–45.

———. "*Viator in Fabula:* Jean-Didier Urbain and the Cultures of Travel in Contemporary France." *Studies in Travel Writing* 4 (2000). 126–140.

Friedman, Susan Stanford. "Exile in the American Grain: H.D.'s Diaspora." *Women's Writing in Exile.* Chapel Hill: University of North Carolina Press, 1989. Mary Lynn Broe and Angela Ingram, eds. 87–112.

Fussell, Paul. *Abroad: British Traveling Between the Wars.* Oxford: Oxford UP, 1980.

Gardiner, Judith Kegan. "The Exhilaration of Exile: Rhys, Stead, and Lessing." *Women's Writing in Exile.* Chapel Hill: University of North Carolina Press, 1989. Mary Lynn Broe and Angela Ingram, eds. 133–150.

Gilbert, Helen, and Anna Johnston. Introduction. *Transit: Travel, Text, Empire.* Ed. Helen Gilbert and Anna Johnston. New York: Peter Lang, 2002. 1–20.

Goulemot, Jean Marie. "Sur les traces des écrivains voyageurs." *Magazine Littéraire* 432 (2004): 22–25.

Gray, Rockwell. "Travel." *Temperamental Journeys: Essays on the Modern Literature of Travel.* Ed. Michael Kowalewski. Athens, GA: University of Georgia, 1992. 33–50.

Grewal, Inderpal. *Home and Harem: Nation, Gender, Empire, and the Cultures of Travel.* Durham: Duke UP, 1996.

Grey, Germaine. "Une grande voyageuse: Ella Maillart." *Minerve* May 1934.

Holland, Patrick, and Graham Huggan. *Tourists with Typewiters: Critical Reflections on Contemporary Travel Writing.* Ann Arbor: U. of Michigan Press, 1998.

Jakubec, Doris. Introduction. *Solitude surpeuplée: Femmes écrivains suisses de langue française.* Ed. Doris Jakubec. Lausanne : Editions d'en bas, 1997.

Jakubec, Doris, ed. *Solitude surpeuplée: Femmes écrivains suisses de langue française.* Lausanne : Editions d'en bas, 1997.

Janson, Deborah. "The Nature of German Romanticism." *Literature of Nature: An International Sourcebook.* Chicago: Fitzroy Dearborn, 1998. Ed. Patrick D. Murphy. 206–212.

Jaton, Anne Marie. "Impressions sur Japon." *Magazine Littéraire* 432 (2004): 55.

Kowalewski, Michael. Introduction. *Temperamental Journeys: Essays on the Modern Literature of Travel.* Ed. Michael Kowalewski. Athens, GA: University of Georgia, 1992. 1–24.

Kravetz, Marc. "L'alternative nomade." *Magazine Littéraire* 432 (2004): 63–4.

Lacarrière, Jacques. "Le Bernard-hermite ou le treizième voyage." *Pour une littérature voyageuse.* Brussels: Editions Complexe, 1999. Alain Borer et al. 105–107.

———. "Hérodote, l'nvention du voyage." *Magazine Littéraire* 432 (2004): 26–27.

Lawrence, Karen. *Penelope Voyages: Women and Travel in the British Literary Tradition.* Ithaca: Cornell UP, 1994.

Leed, Eric. *The Mind of the Traveler: from Gilgamesh to Global Tourism.* New York: Basic Books, 1991.

Leroy, Claude. "Blaise Cendrars, le voyageur à rebours." *Magazine Littéraire* 432 (2004): 52–3.

Linsmayer, Charles. Postface. *La Vallée heureuse.* Annemarie Schwarzenbach. Lausanne : Editions de l'Aire, 1991.129–205.

Loomba, Ania. *Colonialism/ Postcolonialism.* London and New York : Routledge, 1998.

Maillart, Ella. *"Cette réalité que j'ai pourchassée."* Geneva: Zoé, 2003.

———. *Croisières et caravanes.* 1950. Paris: Payot, 1993.

———. *The Cruel Way.* 1947. Boston: Beacon Press, 1986.

———. *Cruises and Caravans.* London: Dent, 1942.

———. *The Forbidden Journey: From Peking to Kashmir.* 1937 Trans. Thomas McGreevy. Evanston, IL: Marlboro Press/ Northwestern University Press, 2003.

———. Letter to Father. May 2, 1930. Ella Maillart Collection. Manuscript Collection, Bibliothèque publique et universitaire, Geneva.

———. *Des Monts célestes aux sables rouges.* 1943. Paris: Payot, 1991.

———. *Gypsy Afloat.* London: William Heinemann, 1942.

———. *The Land of the Sherpas.* London: Hodder and Stoughton, 1955.

———. *Oasis interdites*. 1937. Paris: Payot, 1989.

———. *Parmi la jeunesse russe: de Moscou au Caucase en 1930*. 1932. Lausanne: 24 heures, 1989.

———. *'Ti-Puss*. London: William Heinemann, 1951.

———.*Turkestan Solo*. Trans. John Rodker. London: G.P. Putnam's Sons, 1934.

———. *La Voie cruelle*. 1952. Lausanne: 24 heures, 1987.

———. "Woman's Hour : Ella Maillart." May 2, 1952. Ella Maillart Collection. Radio Emission. Manuscript Collection, Bibliothèque publique et universitaire, Geneva.

Maillart, Ella, and Nicolas Bouvier. *Témoins d'un monde disparu*. Geneva: Zoé, 2002.

———. *La Vie immediate*: photographies / Ella Maillart; textes de Nicolas Bouvier. Lausanne: 24 heures, 1991.

Mantilleri, Brigitte. "Ella Maillart." *Les Femmes dans la mémoire de Genève: Du XVe au XXe siècle*. Eds. Erica Deuber Ziegler and Natalia Tikhonov. Geneva: Editions Suzanne Hurter, 2005. 280–281.

Marcus, Jane. "Alibis and Legends: The Ethics of Elsewhereness, Gender, and Estrange-ment." *Women's Writing in Exile*. Chapel Hill: University of North Carolina Press, 1989. Mary Lynn Broe and Angela Ingram, eds. 269–294.

McColley, Margaret. "The Epistolary Self: Home and Identity in Francophone Women's Travel Letters (1850–1950)." Diss. University of Virginia, 2005.

Miermont, Dominique Laure. *Annemarie Schwarzenbach ou le mal d'Europe*. Paris: Payot, 2004.

Mills, Sara. *Discourses of Difference: An Analysis of Women's Travel Writing and Colonialism*. NY: Routledge, 1991.

Morgan, Susan. *Place Matters: Gendered Geography in Victorian Women's Travel Books about Southeast Asia*. New Brunswick, NJ: Rutgers, 1996.

Morris, Mary. "Women and Journeys: Inner and Outer." *Temperamental Journeys: Essays on the Modern Literature of Travel*. Ed. Michael Kowalewski. Athens, GA: University of Georgia, 1992. 25–32.

Moura, Jean-Marc. "Mémoire culturelle et voyage touristique." *Travel Writing and Cultural Memory / Écriture du voyage et mémoire culturelle*. Ed. Maria Alziro Seixo. *Proceedings of the XVth Congress of the International Comparative Literature Association, August 16–22, 1997*. Vol. 9. Atlanta: Rodopi, 2000. 265–280.

Paes de Barros, Deborah. *Fast Cars and Bad Girls. Nomadic Subjects and Women's Road Stories*. Travel Writing Across the Disciplines 9. New York: Peter Lang, 2004.

Perret, Roger. Afterword. *Où est la terre des promesses? Avec Ella Maillart en Afghanistan (1939–1940)*. 2000. By Annemarie Schwarzenbach. Trans. Dominique Laure Mieremont. Paris: Payot, 2002. 179–195.

Pratt, Mary Louise. "Fieldwork in Common Places." *Writing Culture: The Poetics and Politics of Ethnography*. Berkeley: University of CA, 1986. Eds. James Clifford and George E. Marcus. 27–50.

Pratt, Mary-Louise. *Imperial eyes: Travel Writing and Transculturation*. New York: Routledge, 1992.

Reshtya, Sayed Qasim. "Contemporary Afghanistan–The Last Sixty Years (1919–1979)." *The Price of Liberty: The Tragedy of Afghanistan*. Bardi: Rome, 1984. 31–42. Afghanistan Online. 25 April 2005 <http://www.afghanweb.com/history/articles/reshtya.html>.

Roche, Amandine. *Nomade sur la voie d'Ella Maillart*. Paris: Arthaud, 2003.

Russell, Mary. Introduction. *The Cruel Way*. By Ella Maillart. Boston : Beacon Press, 1986. xiii–xvii.

Said, Edward. *Orientalism*. New York: Vintage, 1979.

———. "Reflections on Exile." *Out There: Marginalization and Contemporary Cultures*. New York: New Museum of Contemporary Art, 1990. Ed. Russell Ferguson et al. 357–366.

Sanchez, Serge. "Nicolas Bouvier, s'immerger dans l'océan du monde." *Magazine Littéraire* 432 (2004): 54–55.

Schwarzenbach, Annemarie. *Dalla parte dell'ombra*. 1990. Trans. Tina D'Agostini. Milano: Saggiatore, 2001.

———. " Dans le jardin des belles jeunes filles de Quaisar." Trans. Dominique Laure Mieremont. *Où est la terre des promesses? Avec Ella Maillart en Afghanistan (1939–1940)*. 2000. Paris: Payot, 2002. 85–90.

———. *Das Glückliche Tal*. Frankfurt am Main: Ullstein, 1991.

———. *La Mort en Perse*. 1995. Trans. Dominique Mieremont. Paris: Payot, 1997.

———. *Orient exils*. 1989. Trans. Dominique Mieremont. Paris: Editions Autrement, 1994.

———. *Où est la terre des promesses? Avec Ella Maillart en Afghanistan (1939–1940)*. 2000. Trans. Dominique Mieremont. Paris: Payot, 2002.

———. "La Steppe. " Trans. Dominique Laure Mieremont.*Où est la terre des promesses? Avec Ella Maillart en Afghanistan (1939–1940)*. 2000. Paris: Payot, 2002. 41–49.

Siegel, Kristi, and Toni B. Wulff. "Travel as Spectacle: The Illusion of Knowledge and Sight." *Issues in Travel Writing: Empire, Spectacle and Displacement*. Ed. Kristi Siegel. New York: Peter Lang, 2002. 109–122.

Smith, Sidonie. *Moving Lives: Twentieth-Century Women's Travel Writing*. Minneapolis: University of Minnesota, 2001.

Sontag, Susan. *On Photography*. New York: Farrar, Strauss, and Giroux, 1977.

Spivak, Gayatri Chakrovorty. "Can the Subaltern Speak?" 1985. *Colonial Discourse and Post-Colonial Theory: A Reader*. Eds. Patrick Williams and Laura Chrisman. New York: Columbia UP, 1994. 66–111.

Stark, Freya. *The Valley of the Assassins*. London: J. Murray, 1936.

Steinert Borella, Sara. "Re-Discovering the Travel Narratives of Ella Maillart." *Women In French Studies* 9 (2001): 123–137.

———. "La Voyageuse, le voyageur et le regard de l'autre : Ella Maillart et Peter Fleming à travers la Chine. " *Agora* 5 (2003): 22–34.

Urbain, Jean-Didier. "*I travel, therefore I am*: The "Nomad Mind" and the Spirit of Travel." Trans. Charles Forsdick. *Studies in Travel Writing* 4 (2000): 141–164.

———. *Secrets de voyage*. Paris: Payot, 1998.

138

Veit, Karin. "Journey and Gender—Diversity in Travel Writing?" *Feminist Contributions to the Literary Canon.* Ed. Susan Fendler. Lewiston: Edwin Mellen, 1997. 109–138.

Weber, Olivier. *Je suis de nulle part ; Sur les traces d'Ella Maillart.* Paris: Payot, 2004.

Whited, Tamara L. "The Mountain in Twentieth-Century French Literature." *Literature of Nature: An International Sourcebook.* Chicago: Fitzroy Dearborn, 1998. Ed. Patrick D. Murphy. 200–205.

Willema, Elvira, ed. *Annemarie Schwarzenbach: Autorin—Reisende—Fotografin.* Pfaffenweiler: Centaurus, 1998.

Williams, Patrick, and Laura Chrisman, eds. *Colonial Discourse and Post-Colonial Theory: A Reader.* New York: Columbia UP, 1994.

"A Woman in Turkestan." Review of *Turkestan Solo,* by Ella Maillart. New York Times 24 Feb. 1935.

Ziegler, Erica Deuber, and Natalia Tikhonov, eds. *Les Femmes dans la mémoire de Genève: Du XVe au XXe siècle.* Geneva: Editions Suzanne Hurter, 2005.

Index

THEORY AND PEDAGOGY
Kristi Siegel, General Editor

The recent critical attention devoted to travel writing enacts a logical transition from the ongoing focus on autobiography, subjectivity, and multiculturalism. Travel extends the inward direction of autobiography to consider the journey outward and intersects provocatively with studies of multiculturalism, gender, and subjectivity. Whatever the journey's motive—tourism, study, flight, emigration, or domination—journey changes both the country visited and the self that travels. *Travel Writing Across the Disciplines* welcomes studies from all periods of literature on the theory and/or pedagogy of travel writing from various disciplines, such as social history, cultural theory, multicultural studies, anthropology, sociology, religious studies, literary analysis, and feminist criticism. The volumes in this series explore journey literature from critical and pedagogical perspectives and focus on travel as metaphor in cultural practice.

For additional information about this series or for the submission of manuscripts, please contact:

Peter Lang Publishing. Inc.
Acquisitions Department
P.O. Box 1246
Bel Air, MD 21014-1246

To order other books in this series, please contact our Customer Service Department:

(800) 770-LANG (within the U.S.)
(212) 647-7706 (outside the U.S.)
(212) 647-7707 FAX

Or browse online by series:
www.peterlangusa.com

DATE DUE
